BEYOND THE BALANCE SHEETS

Unveiling the secret control and implications of various entities for our financial system and our daily lives

By Alessandro Moneta

BEYOND THE BALANCE SHEETS
Unveiling the secret control and implications of various entities for our financial system and our daily lives

Copyright © 2024 by Alessandro Moneta
All rights reserved

No part of this publication may be reproduced, distributed, or transmitted in any form or by any means, including photocopying, recording, or other electronic or mechanical methods, without the prior written permission of the publisher, except in the case of brief quotations embodied in critical reviews and certain other noncommercial uses permitted by copyright law.

This book is a work of non-fiction. It is a result of the author's research and analysis. While the author has made every effort to provide accurate information at the time of publication, the author does not assume and hereby disclaims any liability to any party for any loss, damage, or disruption caused by errors or omissions, whether such errors or omissions result from negligence, accident, or any other cause.

The views and opinions expressed in this book are those of the author and do not necessarily reflect the official policy or position of any agency or organization. The information provided in this book is meant to provide a unique perspective, not investment advice. Readers should consult with a licensed professional before making any financial decisions.

Contact: aleemoneta@gmail.com

**The following subjects will be discussed:
(Feel free to skip parts.)**

Introduction 1

Introduction to BlackRock 4

Objective 7

Part 1

Evolution of money and banking 12

The firsts central banks, how they shaped our economic system? 20

Where does money come from today? 27

A history of capitalism 36

Creation of index funds and their evolution 48

The interconnectedness of our financial system 52

Part 2

How did capitalism, free markets, and private central banking lead to a concentration of wealth and power in the hands of a few entities?........60

Financial stability..65

How one entity could acquire so much wealth: the rise of BlackRock 68

BlackRock's past actions and influence 78

    The 2008 financial crisis....................79

    An adviser for central banks 81

    The pandemic..83

    The FDIC 84

    The war in Ukraine 84

    Investments in China..........................86

    Failure of Signature and Silicon Valley banks 87

    In the Middle East 88

    In Africa 90

Part 3

BlackRock's current magnitude 97

BlackRock's influence on financial markets, and its ability to influence political institutions ... 109

    BlackRock's influence on a company and the whole market 109

    BlackRock's credibility 111

    BlackRock's control over certain domains 112

    Are index funds empty voters? 113

    Why is ESG so popular? 118

    The Engine, Exxon example: how a few firms and ESG can change a board of directors 123

    BlackRock's influence on political elections 125

    BlackRock's little-known influence on central banks 126

To conclude 128

BlackRock's influence on social and economic inequality 129

    Different interests 131

    Aladdin's Monopoly 134

    Inequality on asset price inflation 135

    To conclude 136

Part 4

What role could BlackRock play in the future? 141

    Future growth 142

    The emerging problems 146

Possible solutions 152

    What can we do? Are there solutions which would enable us to stay in a capitalist economy and a liberal democracy? 152

An alternative point of view............ 158

Conclusion

A few things to remember........................... 166

Acknowledgement... 170

References 172

Introduction

I have always been interested in our world, particularly our economic system, not from a theoretical perspective but more from a practical standpoint. Of course, with that comes a curiosity about money: how it works, where it comes from, who controls it, who creates it, and how it is built. However, as I delved deeper into the topic, I realised that it is much more complex than it initially seemed. I read a lot, and I found it hard to find books that explain our financial system in a way an ordinary person can relate to or at least comprehend. To answer my simple questions, I decided to research and write about it. I'm a very curious.

Quickly, you realise that some entities manage money for a huge amount of people. Most people store their money in banks, pension funds, hedge funds[1], and mutual funds[2] nowadays, but what do these institutions do with

---

[1] A hedge fund is a limited partnership of private investors whose money is pooled and managed by professional fund managers. These managers use a wide range of strategies, including leverage (borrowed money) and the trading of non-traditional assets, to earn above-average investment returns.

[2] A mutual fund is an investment program funded by shareholders that trades in diversified holdings. It pools money from many investors to buy a variety of stocks, bonds, or other securities. This allows individuals to diversify their investments

Introduction

the money? Do they invest it in the stock market or buy bonds? Yes, most do. But then, If the company receives money from their stocks, what does it do with it? Do they give it again to banks to store it? Where does the money end up? Where does it come from? How do banks have access to it? Where does money flow to, and how? Finally, who has the most control over it?

When researching the flow of money, I looked at central banks and big investment firms, which are a great starting point. I often heard the word "BlackRock" when doing this research. Therefore, out of curiosity, I decided to research this name, and I discovered that it is the most significant investment fund in the world, managing over 10 trillion dollars in assets as of the end of 2021 and a bit less, around 9.5 trillion in 2023. Aladdin, its risk management tool, which managed over 20 trillion dollars in assets in 2017 (no newer data available), including a big part of BlackRock assets. To put that into perspective; America's GDP[3] was 26 trillion in 2023. Learning about BlackRock's immense funds triggered questions in me.

---

and access a broader range of strategies or assets than they might be able to on their own.

[3] Gross Domestic Product (GDP) is the total monetary or market value of all finished goods and services produced within a country's borders in a specific period.

Introduction

With such funds, could they manipulate markets, influence our behaviours, speculate on prices, and decide which industries flourish or fail? BlackRock assets, representing almost half of the GDP of the world's most powerful country, piqued my interest in big investment firms and the potential ramifications of a single entity controlling so much wealth. Therefore, a big part of my research is dedicated to BlackRock.

That one entity can manage so much money, and nobody even speaks about it is shocking. I had to find out more. I decided to focus on BlackRock because it's the most significant investment firm by AUM[4] (assets under management). However, I will also discuss other significant firms and entities.

---

[4] Assets Under Management (AUM) is the total market value of investments managed by a person or entity on behalf of clients. It includes bank deposits, mutual funds, and cash, and fluctuates with fund flows and asset performance.

Introduction

Introduction to BlackRock

BlackRock is a global investment management company founded in 1988. Larry Fink was its principal founder and is now its Chairman and CEO. He owns, as of January 2023, 520,126 shares[5] in BlackRock, less than 1 percent. BlackRock's global headquarters are located in New York City, but it has offices in more than 35 countries worldwide, including China, the Middle East, Africa and Europe. BlackRock has over 10 trillion dollars in assets under management as of December 2021. The company offers a wide range of investment solutions to institutions, financial professionals, and individuals worldwide. BlackRock is also a leading risk management, investment analytics, and advisory services provider.

Most of us have some money invested in BlackRock, either directly via our investments in their funds (mostly their Exchange-Traded Funds[6]) or stock, or indirectly via

---

[5] Shares are units of ownership in a company or financial asset. They are sold to investors and traders to raise capital for the company. The terms "shares" and "stocks" are often used interchangeably.

[6] An ETF will track the performance of a particular index. It can be a group of stocks, commodities, or a collection of securities. They are like mutual funds. The main difference is

Introduction

our pension funds or our bank where we deposit our money, and they invest our money in BlackRock's funds. The investments of a company as big as BlackRock affect all of us. We are all impacted by their investment decisions. It is important to understand that BlackRock is not a bank. Therefore, it is not regulated like a bank. It is subject to fewer requirements and can't lend money to its clients. It is an investment firm. It can only invest, but as we will see, its investments have an undeniable influence.

I will show you how, even if you think you are not affected by BlackRock, the contrary may be true. But first, let's go back and understand a bit of history.

BlackRock is a public company. In the following graph, we can see its 10 largest shareholders.

---

that they can be traded on a stock exchange like you would buy a regular stock and that the fees are generally lower.

Introduction

Top 10 biggest shareholders of BlackRock as of 2023.

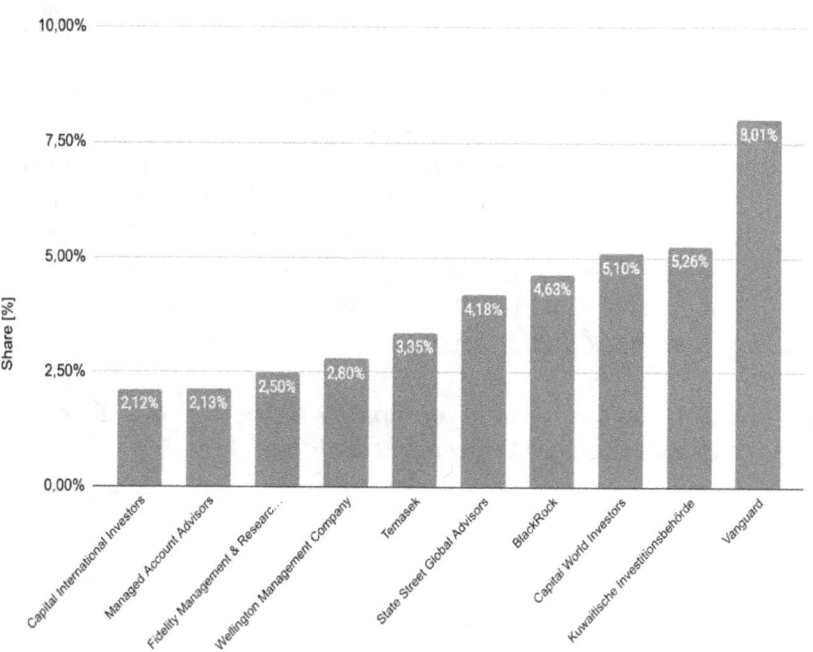

Data: Spotlight on BlackRock

Book plan

Objective

(This book was finished and reviewed last in April of 2024. The situation may be worsening since then.)

Part 1:
First, I will delve deep into our financial system, trying to understand how banks were created and the creation of the first central bank. I will also speak about the rise of capitalism, the creation of the first hedge funds, and the money creation process.

Part 2:
I will then reveal how this paved the way for the economic situation we are in today. One where some entities control too much wealth, where all our financial institutions are connected. I will speak about the stability of our system and about BlackRock, delving into its success story and past influences on the world.

Part 3:
Additionally, I will discuss BlackRock's magnitude, its current influence on political and financial institutions and social and economic inequality.

Part 4:
Finally, I will discuss the future, what could happen, and the interventions to prevent our financial system from destroying itself.

Book plan

My concrete example will be BlackRock. However, it is comparable to other huge entities such as Vanguard or State Street. During this research, I will try not to give an opinion. However, if I do, it will be argued with facts. This is not a study trying to prove what I think. I discovered facts, wrote them down, explained them and made connections. The most significant part of my research was conducted through the analysis on the internet of financial articles, documentaries, and books. I tried to interview someone working at BlackRock to get their opinion on the matter but did not receive a response to my request.

My main objective with this book is to raise awareness of a problem that most of us have never previously heard about. I hope that everyone who reads this book will understand a little more about our economic system and the flow of money. I would like people to realise that there is a difference between how our economic system should work theoretically and how it works practically.

At the bottom of the pages, there are a few definitions. If there are words you do not understand, I would recommend looking at them.

Part 1:

The starting point: where does our financial system come from?

Part 1: Where does our financial system come from?

Evolution of money and banking

When did money first appear? Before the advent of specialization, humans had little need for money. In small tribal societies, people relied on mutual aid, expecting that their assistance would be reciprocated in the future. However, as kingdoms and cities emerged, populations became denser, and individuals began to concentrate on their unique skills. This allowed them to trade their specialized services or products with others who had different skills.

As cities grew more populous, the potential for specialization increased. However, this led to a problem: if a butcher trades meat for corn, what happens when the corn seller no longer needs meat? How can the corn seller determine the worth of his corn in terms of meat? The butcher must be able to offer something that the corn seller wants, and they both must agree on the value of the trade.

This necessitated a universal commodity that everyone desired and agreed to trade for, which could be used to price goods. This commodity was at first precious metals, with time it evolved into what we now know as money, a universally accepted medium of exchange that today has no real worth. Money solved the problem of direct barter by providing a common measure of value, making trade more efficient and flexible.

Yuval Noah Harari author of *Sapiens* gives a great definition of money: "Money is not coins and banknotes. Money is anything that people are willling to use in order

Part 1: Where does our financial system come from?

to represent systematicallly the value of other things for the purpose of exchanging goods ans services."

Money, as we have understood it, is a construct of our collective imagination. It appears tangible because of the widespread belief in its existence and value. However, money itself holds no intrinsic[7] value. If you were to travel to another planet, your money would be worthless, as the inhabitants would likely not recognize or use the same currency.

For a currency to function effectively, it must be widely accepted and used. But why would anyone use something that holds no inherent value? The answer lies in trust. Money may not possess tangible value, but the mutual trust that citizens place in it has facilitated the creation of a system where money is used as a medium of exchange. We trust in the value of money, knowing that we can exchange it for goods at the supermarket. Consequently, we accept payment in the form of money for our labour.

This mutual trust is pivotal for the functioning of money. If we trace the evolution of money through time, we can observe how this trust has gradually solidified. The earliest known form of money dates back to around 3000 BC in Sumer, where barley grains were used as currency. Barley has intrinsic value; it can be consumed as food. As

---

[7] Intrinsic value refers to the inherent worth of an asset based on its tangible qualities and utility. On the other hand, perceived value, is the worth that a product or service has in the mind of the consumer.

Part 1: Where does our financial system come from?

trust in the system grew, precious metals, which hold no inherent value, began to be used as money. Precious metals like silver are considered valuable not because of their rarity, but because we attribute a perceived value to them.

For instance, consider Helium-3, a rare isotope of helium present on Earth in extremely small quantities. Despite its rarity, it holds no value because it currently has no utility and there is no demand for it.

The use of silver, a material with no inherent value, as a form of currency was a significant step that demonstrated the deepening trust our ancestors had in money. However, the most monumental breakthrough occurred in the 13th century in China when the government issued banknotes not backed by any precious metal or commodity - the birth of fiat money[8]. For the first time, money was entirely backed by trust in the issuer. Fiat money did not become the dominant form of currency until the 20th century when a significant shift occurred in 1971. U.S. President Richard Nixon decided to suspend the convertibility of the

---

[8] The word "fiat" originated from Latin, specifically from the phrase "fiat lux" which means "let there be light" in the book of Genesis. The usage of fiat money in an economy is a practical application of its definition. It exists and has value because the government commands it to be so, and because the people using it trust this command. If this trust were to falter, the money would lose its value, demonstrating the inherent risk and reliance on mutual trust in a fiat money system.

Part 1: Where does our financial system come from?

U.S. dollar to gold, leading to the global adoption of a system of national fiat currencies. Today, most of the money in circulation is fiat money.

Looking forward, we might see a shift towards digital currencies, existing solely on the Blockchain. The physical dollar bill, with "In God We Trust" inscribed on it, could be replaced by digital numbers. Instead of trusting a physical entity, we would need to trust our internet connection and computer systems.

The concept of universal money has enabled the creation of an international financial system where everyone cooperates for a common objective – gaining money, a feat no other fictional idea could have achieved.

The reverse of a United States twenty-dollar bill, capitalized: "IN GOD WE TRUST"

Source: Wikipedia Commons

Part 1: Where does our financial system come from?

Grasping the evolution of money is scratching the surface of the transformation our financial system has undergone. To truly comprehend the entirety of this evolution, one must delve into the realm of banking. Over time, banking has morphed into a system deeply rooted in usury, perpetuating an endless cycle of money multiplication.

Banking throughout the years has completely changed. Initially, banks were created when the first currencies were issued, and people realised they needed a place to store their money. At first, people stored their money in temples because they were seen as safe places, and most people trusted them. However, the banking system, as we know, grew in Italy during the Renaissance. The Medici Family, who were merchants, were the first to create a double-entry bank in 1397 in Florence, meaning that the equation: "Assets = Liabilities + Equity"[9] was created and that the credit and the debit of the merchants were

---

[9] The equation Assets = Liabilities + Equity is the cornerstone of double-entry accounting. It represents a company's financial position by showing what it owns (assets), owes (liabilities), and the value belonging to shareholders (equity). This equation ensures that every business transaction is accurately recorded and balanced, thereby serving as a critical tool for financial decision-making and analysis. Its importance lies in its ability to provide a clear snapshot of a company's financial health at any given time.

Part 1: Where does our financial system come from?

recorded. From there on, merchants had a precise overview of their business's accounts and could make smarter decisions. The Medicis also introduced the letter of credit, an agreement stating that the bank where the merchant has an account will pay back the seller when the merchant receives the goods that he bought. It was quite a simple thing, but it was vital at that time because it was too dangerous to ship money abroad, so letters of credit were used to enable the safe transfer of money between the buyer and the seller. Because of that, international trade grew much faster. Then, the Medici slowly started to charge interest rates for these letters (very similar to our banking system). Many of these services (deposits, lending, exchange, interests) now form the bases of banking today.

However, the most significant changes in the banking system have occurred in the last 100-200 years, when the first central banks were established. A new era started when the Federal Reserve, the central bank of the United States, was founded in 1913. There were already other central banks in Europe, such as the Bank of England or the Bank of France, but the Federal Reserve is the one that plays the most crucial role, because of the strength of the United States. As the Federal Reserve states: "It was created by the Congress to provide the nation with a safer, more flexible, and more stable monetary and financial system." Central banks were created to provide financial stability. One of their main roles was to manage the gold standard (the exchange of a fixed weight of gold for the currency of a country. Their focus was primarily on price

Part 1: Where does our financial system come from?

stability. It changed after WW1 when central banks started to focus on the stability of the real economy (output, unemployment, prices).

This evolution or creation of a central banking system heavily affected the development of commercial banks. Firstly, there was now a lender of last resort: the central bank, providing liquidity[10] to banks during bad times. It was essential because it helped maintain confidence in commercial banks even in financial distress, so people trusted banks more with their money. Central banks also supervised commercial banks, enforcing regulations about excessive risk-taking and capital requirements, promoting stability. This way, depositors felt safe. Today, most people trust banks with their money, even their pension funds. Central banks regularly check the financial situation of commercial banks to be sure they comply with these measures and that they are not doing whatever they can to boost their profits. They have become key to our economy. Finally, central banks implement monetary policies, mainly interest rates, which significantly impact commercial banks, boosting their lending activity or slowing it down.

Recently, there has been an evolution in digital currency. Central banks are trying to create a new form of money, called CBDCs, Central Bank Digital Currency. They are

---

[10] In the context of a bank, liquidity refers to the availability of cash or assets that can be quickly converted into cash to meet deposit withdrawals and other financial obligations.

Part 1: Where does our financial system come from?

supported by central banks and powered by blockchain, offering prospects of improved efficiency, security, and financial inclusivity. Currently, about 100 nations are investigating the use of CBDCs. They could provide more resilience, security, accessibility, and affordability compared to private digital currencies. Furthermore, they have the potential to incorporate the entire population into the banking system, leading to cost savings and increased efficiency. The concept is still very new, but it is important to mention it in this section because if CBDCs are used in most places then commercial banks will lose most of their utility. We will then be navigating on a complete digital financial system. Therefore, there are a few concerns about them such as the potential to heighten the monitoring of financial activities, leading to issues related to privacy and security, and the fact that they would provide the government with transactional data and a lot of user information.

One might ask, but then, when, and where does the usury of banking come into play? To fully grasp this concept, we must turn our attention to the Bank of England. It served as the blueprint for all subsequent central banks that were established in its wake. It is this very bank that pioneered a system rooted in perpetual usury.

Part 1: Where does our financial system come from?

The firsts central banks, how they shaped our economic system?

The first central bank globally came into existence in 1668 as the Swedish Riksbank, established by Sweden's parliament, the Riksdag. Operating as a joint stock[11] bank, it was granted authorization to provide financial assistance to the government and function as a clearing house for commercial activities. It played a role in ensuring the efficient processing of financial transactions between various participants in the economy, ensuring that funds were transferred securely and accurately between different entities involved in commercial activities. In essence, the Riksbank played a crucial role in facilitating financial transactions and extending government loans[12].

The establishment of the Riksbank signalled the commencement of central banking, introducing the

---

[11] A joint stock company is a business organisation where ownership is divided into shares that can be bought and sold, enabling multiple individuals or entities to hold a proportional stake in the company's assets and liabilities.

[12] Refers to financial assistance or credit extended by the Riksbank to the government. These loans could be utilised by the government to finance various projects, cover budgetary needs, or address economic challenges.

Part 1: Where does our financial system come from?

concept of an institution dedicated to overseeing a nation's currency, monetary policies, and financial stability. The distinct categorisation of central banks, separate from other financial institutions, such as banks, evolved gradually and solidified only in the 20th century.

Several decades later, in 1694, the Bank of England was established, operating similarly to the Swedish Riksbank as a joint stock company. However, its primary purpose was to acquire government debt.

Royal Charter founded the Bank of England following the Glorious Revolution of 1688. William III of Orange and Queen Mary ascended to the throne following the revolution. The country's financial situation wasn't good; they had to come up with a solution. William III desperately tried to find funds for the Nine Years War against Louis XIV.

Sir William Paterson, a Scottish trader and banker, proposed to finance the government debt by private subscriptions of individual shareholders[13]. He wrote a description of it entitled "A Brief Account of the Intended Bank of England" He says the following: "The want of a

---

[13] Shareholders are individuals or entities that own shares or equity in a company. By holding shares, shareholders become partial owners of the company and have a financial interest in its performance. Shareholders may receive dividends as a share of the company's profits and typically have the right to vote on certain corporate decisions at shareholder meetings.

Part 1: Where does our financial system come from?

Bank, or publick Fund, for the convenience and se-curity of great Payments, and the better to facilitate the circulation of Money, in and about this great and oppulent City, hath in our time, among other Inconve-niencies, occasion'd much unnecessary Credit, to the loss of several Millions, by which Trade hath been exceedingly discourag'd and obstru-cted", "This, together with the height of Inte-rest or Forbearance of Money, which for some time past hath born no manner of proportion—to that of our Rival Neighbors, and for which no tolerable Reason could ever be given either in Notion or Practise, considering the Riches and Trade of England, unless it were the want of publick Funds; by which the Effects of the Nation, in some sort, might be disposed to an-swer the Use, and do the Office of Money, and become more useful to the Trade and Im-provements thereof".

Paterson proposed to loan £1.2 million to the Crown, the equivalent of around £220 million today, with 8% interest per annum. The £1.2 million was raised in just 11 days by 1,268 members of the public and were formally established by Royal Charter on 27 July 1694. Thus, the Crown or the government would have to pay £100'000 in interest per year to the shareholders of the Bank, (the extra £4000 was an administrative fee).

Part 1: Where does our financial system come from?

"Sealing of the Bank of England Royal Charter [14] 1694"

---

[14] A legal document issued by the monarch or government, outlining the establishment and authority of the bank. The charter specifies the bank's purpose, structure, rights, and responsibilities, essentially serving as a foundational legal framework for the institution. The act of sealing the charter involves affixing the monarch's or authorised official's seal to the document, symbolising formal approval and recognition of the institution's existence and functions.

Part 1: Where does our financial system come from?

Source: Alice Archer Houblon, The Houblon Family, vol. 1, 1907

Part 1: Where does our financial system come from?

The bill passed to create the Bank of England introduced complicated rates, duties, and taxes on ships, beer, ale, and other liquors. These taxes were used to raise funds for the war with France. To be more accurate, these taxes were needed to fund the interest on future government loans. The least productive one introduced in 1799 was the income tax not only on companies but even on workers, again to fund interest on debt for wars. From 1793 to the Battle of Waterloo in June 1815, the Napoleonic Wars cost Britain more than £1,650,000,000. The cost of the wars in today's money would be approximately £18,116,698,000,000 (or over 18 trillion pounds). Do not forget that a large part of this sum was debt with interest rates, which compounded each year, some of it until today. England created an ingenious system to create money out of nothing; with that, it could fund wars that would have been impossible to fund. The British Empire became one of the largest empires in history, and Britain became the global power in the 19th century. However, the consequence of this system was and still is the perpetual enslavement of people with never-ending interest rates that enrich private investors.

The Bank of England became the model on which all subsequent central banks were replicated, and how central banks work today is largely due to The Bank of England.
    Mayer Amschel Rothschild, the founder of the Rothschild banking dynasty, is famously credited with having said: "Give me control of the economics of a country, and I care not who makes her laws. The few who

Part 1: Where does our financial system come from?

understand the system, will either be so interested from its profits or so dependent on its favours, that there will be no opposition from that class."

His son, Nathan Mayer Rothschild, controlled the Bank of England by 1815. He declared: "I care not what puppet is placed upon the throne of England to rule the Empire on which the sun never sets. The man who controls Britain's money supply controls the British Empire, and I control the British money supply."

Part 1: Where does our financial system come from?

Where does money come from today?

Let's go back to the question of how money is created today, in this private owned central banking system. We have seen that money is fictional, but if you haven't understood yet, money is created out of nothing on interest we must pay, let me explain. Most of the money in our economy is created by banks in the form of bank deposits. The central banks are the ones deciding if the economy needs more money to be created or not. The central banks look at the economy. In bad times, they will tend to pump the economy with new money; in good times, they will tend to shrink the money supply.

When the central banks want to pump the money supply, the most common method is to trade available treasury bonds[15] in the market for newly created money.
    Christopher Leonard explains this very well in his book, *The Lords of Easy Money,* which I highly recommend: "From the terminal, the Fed trader put out a bid on a

---

[15] Treasury bonds are long-term debt securities issued by a government, specifically the U.S. Department of the Treasury in the case of the United States. Investors purchase these bonds, essentially lending money to the government, in exchange for periodic interest payments and the return of the principal amount upon maturity.

Part 1: Where does our financial system come from?

specific asset— like long-term Treasury bonds or mortgage-backed securities[16]— then waited to see which primary dealer was willing to sell, at the best price.

The Fed always drew bids for its auction for a simple reason: It was the most powerful buyer in the world. It could simply create however much money it needed to close a deal. When the Fed and J. P. Morgan agreed on a price, say $10 billion for a bunch of Treasury bonds, for example, then the trader at J. P. Morgan would send its Treasury bonds to the Fed. This was the moment when the Fed trader entered a few keystrokes at the computer terminal and created the money for the transaction.

When the J. P. Morgan trader checked the balance of the bank's reserve account at the Fed, 10 billion new dollars had appeared to fund the transaction. **This is how the Fed created money on Wall Street. It took in an asset, and paid for it by making new dollars inside the reserve accounts of primary dealers.** [...] The primary dealers were not just selling the Treasury bills and mortgage bonds that they happened to have on hand. If that had been the case, it would have limited how much money the Fed could have pushed into the banking system (even the primary dealers only had a finite amount of such assets on hand). Instead, the Fed set up a conveyor belt of sorts,

---

[16] Securities are financial instruments that represent ownership in a company (equity securities, such as stocks) or a creditor relationship with a governmental body or a corporation (debt securities, such as bonds).

Part 1: Where does our financial system come from?

which used the primary dealers as middlemen. The conveyor belt began outside the Fed, with hedge funds that were not primary dealers. These hedge funds could borrow money from a big bank, buy a Treasury bill, and then have a primary dealer sell that Treasury bill to the Fed for new cash. In this way, the hedge funds could borrow and buy billions of dollars in bonds, and sell them to the Fed for a profit. Once the conveyor belt was up and running, it began magically transforming bonds into cash. The cash didn't stay safe and sound inside the reserve accounts of primary dealers. It started flowing out into the banking system, looking for a place to live."

When central banks want to shrink the money supply, they do the opposite: they sell Treasury bonds, taking money out of the economy, so money becomes more expensive to borrow, and interest rates hike.

All this newly printed money is digital. Money doesn't have to be printed physically. About 97% of the money in circulation is in the form of digital bank deposits (numbers on a bank account), and 3% is physical cash. Let's return to what Christopher Leonard briefly mentioned: what happens after the money enters the bank?

Additionally, there is something else that is called "a fractional reserve banking system". It means the following: if the central banks decide to add 100 billion to the market, nearly 100 billion will enter bank reserves, but because of fractional reserve banking, banks are not legally required to hold all the money they lend. In Switzerland, banks currently need to have about 2.5% of

Part 1: Where does our financial system come from?

the money they lend on hand. So, from that 100 billion, banks will create new loans and fill the market with over a trillion. Therefore, banks also create money when they create loans through fractional banking. As loans are repaid and new deposits are created, the process continues, leading to an expansion of the money supply.

   The following image illustrates an example of how fast the money supply can grow through fractional reserve banking and how interconnected our financial system is. When a person decides to buy a house and doesn't have the full amount to pay for it, they approach a bank for a loan. The bank, in turn, can grant this loan if it meets the reserve requirement. Once the loan is approved, the buyer can then purchase the house. The seller of the house receives the payment, which they typically deposit into their bank account. Now, the money is back in the banking system. The seller's bank can then lend out the majority of this deposited money to other customers, keeping only a small portion as reserves. This cycle can continue almost indefinitely, with the bank repeatedly lending out most of the deposited money, while always retaining the required reserves. The formula to calculate, the entirety of the money that enters the market is the money multiplier formula, it is a reciprocal function such as $\frac{1}{x}$. A small difference in the reserve requirement has a significant impact on how much money enters the market. It is a simplified example, some other factors may have to be considered such as the demand for loans, and the bank's willingness to lend.

Part 1: Where does our financial system come from?

Money creation through fractional reserve banking. How one thousand dollars become forty thousand dollars?

Part 1: Where does our financial system come from?

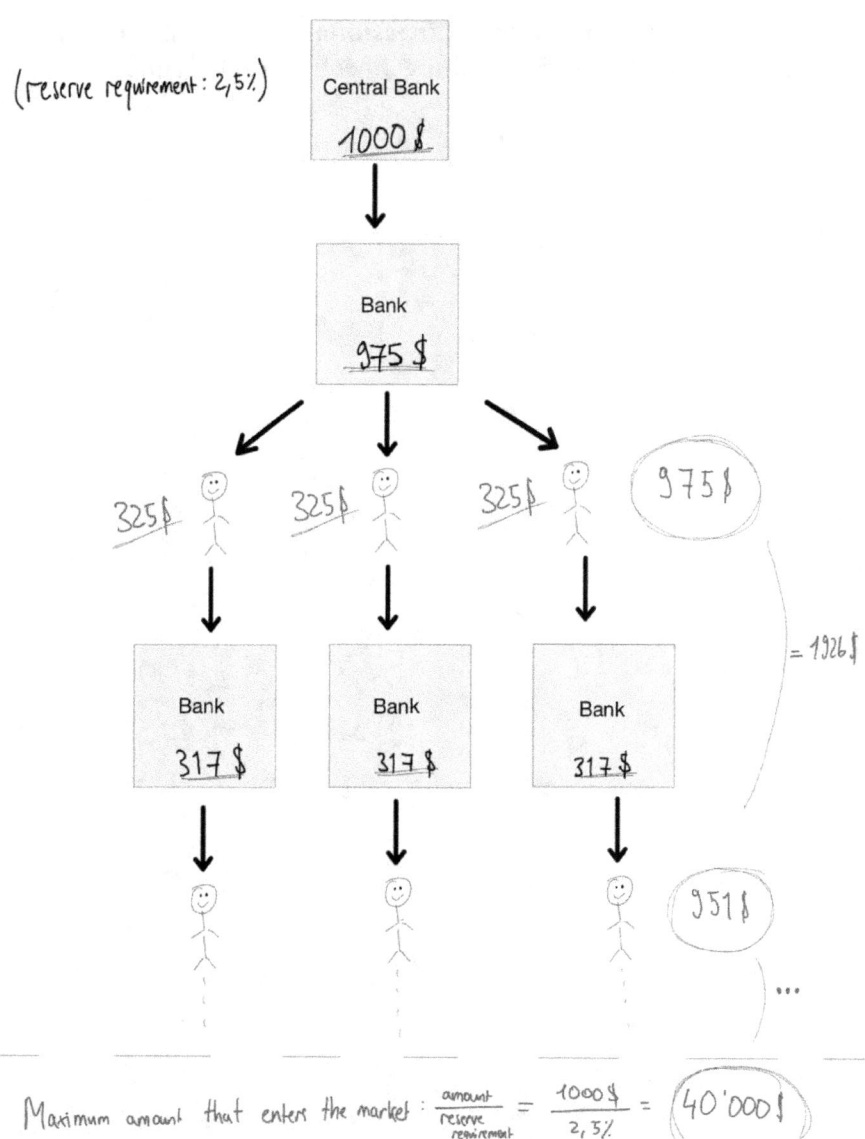

Part 1: Where does our financial system come from?

Pretty much the same can happen in reverse. For example, let's say there's a bank named Bank A which has $1 million in its reserve. John wants to build a house that costs approximately $1 million, so he goes to Bank A and asks for a loan. Bank A agrees and credits a loan of $1 million to John's account (Bank A creates the $1 million).

John then makes a payment to the builder, Bob, who deposits this money in his account at the same bank, Bank A. Now, Bank A still has $1 million in its reserve. But Bob also has also $1 million in his account.

A year later, John's family grows, and he wants a bigger house. Bob says he can make it bigger for an additional $1 million. John goes back to Bank A and asks for another loan of $1 million. Bank A agrees and credits another $1 million to John's account.

John pays Bob again, and Bob deposits this money in his account at Bank A. Now, Bob has $2 million in his bank account, but Bank A still has the same $1 million in its reserve from the beginning.

So, where does that extra 2 million in Bob's account come from?

This is where the concept of fractional banking comes in. Bank A has essentially created the extra $2 million through fractional banking. With a reserve requirement of 2.5%, Bank A can continue to do this more than 7 times, creating more money in the economy while still only having $1 million in its actual reserve. If John wanted to withdraw his $2 million at once it would be a serious problem for Bank A.

Part 1: Where does our financial system come from?

However, to understand the whole system of money creation, it is crucial to also understand the impact of interest rates on the economy and vice-versa. In periods of low or even negative interest rates, banks are compelled to explore higher-yield investment options due to the excess money in circulation. Bond yields typically tend to be lower, and there is a risk of rapid inflation. As a result, people may find their savings are worth less and less, acting as a disincentive to saving. Hence, they might resort to riskier investments, basically anything with a return higher than zero.

An example of this was when the FED, the US central bank, pushed interest rates close to zero after the financial crisis in 2008. As Christopher Leonard observes in his book: "In early 2012, the richest one percent of America owned about 25 percent of all assets. The bottom half of all Americans owned only 6.5 per cent of all assets. When the Fed stocked asset prices, it was helping a vanishingly small group of people at the top." Most people at the top had their money invested in assets with better returns than the actual interest rates. Investment firms, such as BlackRock, which weren't regulated as much as banks, and could take far more risks and thus propose the desired return to their customers, were very successful. Others, afraid of the financial crisis, were saving money for the uncertain future. Because of the low-interest rate, people saving money were penalising themselves.

Any fund or investment company could make an enormous amount of money during those times. Christopher Leonard says in his book: "Very few hedge-

Part 1: Where does our financial system come from?

fund operators seemed eager to complain about the way that ZIRP widened income inequality and fueled speculative bubbles." (ZIRP = zero interest rate policy.)

However, when central banks tighten the money supply, the opposite happens: asset bubbles burst, people panic and take their money out of their investments or bank deposit accounts. Because of fractional reserve banking, the bank doesn't have that money, so it must cash out on its investment to gain liquidity. Often, in bad times, these investments are losses, so the bank loses a lot of money, sometimes leading to bank failure.

While this explanation may not be taking every factor into account, it provides an understanding of the origins of money and the ripple effects it creates upon entering the market. Most importantly, it underscores the central bank's power and importance in supervising our economic system. It's crucial to remember that these central banks are privately owned. Private shareholders exert influence over their decisions, striving to maximize their profits at every possibility. After all, isn't that the essence of a capitalist system? As we transition into the next chapter, we will delve deeper into the history of capitalism itself and understand its roots.

Part 1: Where does our financial system come from?

A history of capitalism

The genesis of the capitalist economic model is deeply rooted in historical transformations spanning centuries and influenced by a myriad of interconnected factors.

Before the advent of capitalism, the medieval era was characterized by feudalism, a system that was defined by a hierarchical social structure. This structure was centered around land ownership and the obligations of labor.

During this period, people's outlook on the future was generally pessimistic. Their thoughts were often consumed by immediate concerns, such as the possibility of the next drought or rainfall. The prevalent mindset was one of apprehension about the future, with most people expecting conditions to worsen rather than improve.

This pessimism was largely due to their perception of the economy. They viewed the money supply as a fixed quantity, incapable of growth. Consequently, they believed that the economic "pie" remained constant in size, and any changes would merely involve dividing it into different-sized portions, rather than increasing the overall size. This mindset made it difficult for them to envision a future where conditions could improve.

The subsequent emergence of mercantilism during the Renaissance, an economic theory and practice common in Europe from the 16th to the 18th century, played a significant role in the development of trust in the future and therefore, of capitalism. Strong national states grew during that era. Precious metals were essential for a

Part 1: Where does our financial system come from?

nation's wealth and had to be attained by trade or mined in colonies. Mercantilists believed in having more exports than imports. The mercantilist strategy used colonies to export goods and obtain raw materials for the mother country. This approach led to these states' adoption of uniform monetary systems and legal codes, promoting governmental regulation of a nation's economy. People believed that being careful with money, saving, and not spending too much were good qualities. They thought these habits were the key to creating wealth. These ideas from mercantilism created a positive environment for the early development of capitalism, which promised the opportunity for potential profits. The East India Companies, companies engaging in trade in the Indian Ocean region, were provided charters[17] by the British, French, and Dutch as part of their plan to increase their exports. These companies pioneered the issuance of shares that yielded dividends[18] from the total earnings of

---

[17] These charters granted the company exclusive trading rights, privileges, and defined its powers and responsibilities to overseas trade, particularly in the East Indies. The charters played a crucial role in shaping the structure and authority, of the East India Company during the colonial era.

[18] A payment made by a corporation to its shareholders as a distribution of profits. It is typically paid out regularly and represents a portion of the company's earnings. Dividends are a way for shareholders to receive a share of the company's profits

Part 1: Where does our financial system come from?

all expeditions, instead of individual trips. This innovation marked the birth of the first modern joint-stock companies. It was there the beginning of trust in a better future – the first investments in the future. Investments provided credits to finance the trips, the trips provided new colonies, the colonies provided profits to the investor. As a result, they could set higher prices for their shares and expand their fleets. The substantial size of these corporations, coupled with royal decrees that prohibited competition, ensured profitable returns for shareholders.

Mercantilism, by fostering trade, generating capital, and bolstering domestic industries, laid the groundwork for the shift towards capitalism. However, economic inequality rose and was justified by the idea that the wealthy were more virtuous than the poor. Later, mercantilism was significantly criticised. The critics argued for the self-regulation of money supply, believing that the money a state would need could exist in excess (higher amount than there is demand for) and opposed the idea that a nation could only prosper by exploiting others, challenging mercantilism with alternative economic ideas.

These critics laid the basic foundations for capitalism and free markets. In fact, one can accumulate wealth not by depriving others, but by contributing to the growth of the economy.

---

and are often seen as a form of return on investment for those holding the company's stock.

Those are the ideas of one of the most important economists of all times – the father of modern economics – Adam Smith.

Adam Smith (1787 portrait by James Tassie)

At the same time the Agricultural Revolution of the 18th century marked a pivotal shift with improved farming techniques, leading to population growth and the release of labour for alternative economic pursuits. The Industrial

Part 1: Where does our financial system come from?

Revolution that followed, characterised by mechanised production in factories, further accelerated economic transformation. Exploration and colonisation expanded trade networks globally, fostering the exchange of goods and ideas. Philosophical and intellectual changes during the Enlightenment, notably articulated by thinkers like John Locke and Adam Smith. John Locke defined property as the product of labour, he defended wealth accumulation and accepted inequality resulting from it. Adam Smith in 1776 published *The Wealth of Nations*. The same year as the American Declaration of Independence was issued. His ideas were revolutionary at that time. Here are some of his most important ideas in his own words, just to state a few:

- "Man is an animal that makes bargains: no other animal does this — no dog exchanges bones with another."
- "All money is a matter of belief."
- "It is not from the benevolence of the butcher, the brewer, or the baker that we expect our dinner, but from their regard to their own interest".
- "A nation is not made wealthy by the childish accumulation of shiny metals, but it enriched by the economic prosperity of its people".

Adam Smith's ideas, while commonplace today, were revolutionary during his time when capitalism was still a nascent concept. One of his groundbreaking propositions was that an individual earning profits beyond what is

Part 1: Where does our financial system come from?

necessary for his sustenance would reinvest the surplus. This reinvestment, often in the form of employing others, would therefore stimulate job creation and contribute to the overall economy. The economic 'pie' was not a fixed entity anymore but could expand indefinitely with the right conditions.

This interpretation aligns with Smith's concepts of self-interest, where individuals pursuing their own economic interests inadvertently benefit society at large.

Finally, the inception of Gross Domestic Product (GDP) as a measure of a nation's economic activity can be traced back to the pioneering work of William Petty. Since its introduction, nations worldwide have strived relentlessly to maximize this figure, equating economic growth to a mere numerical value. Regrettably, this single-minded pursuit of GDP growth overlooks a critical aspect – the well-being of the population. GDP, in its current form, fails to account for the holistic welfare of a nation's citizens, thus presenting an incomplete picture of a country's true economic health.

Those big changes brought a new perspective to the economy, beyond a perspective they brought a system – capitalism. These ideas were the foundation on which modern economic theory and the capitalist system were built.

Those developments happened just a little later after the creation of the Bank of England. The Bank of England and other financial institutions facilitated the necessary capital for industrial growth, thus playing a significant role in this economic transformation, characterised by the growth of

Part 1: Where does our financial system come from?

industries, the expansion of trade, and the development of financial institutions, such as the creation of the stock exchange in London in 1773 and then the New York Stock Exchange in 1792. After the French Revolution and the Napoleonic Wars, the old system of feudalism was completely wiped out, and the few countries that still had a state-owned banking system were abolished. This paved the way for Adam Smith's economic theories to be implemented more widely. Smith's ideas, which were the basis for 19th-century political liberalism, included principles like free trade, sound money (a stable form of money, in this case backed by gold), balanced budgets, and basic levels of support for the poor.

This led to the rise of industrial capitalism and the development of factories during the 19th century. A new class of industrial workers emerged, living in poor conditions.

This harsh reality inspired the revolutionary ideas of Karl Marx, in his book *Capital: A Critique of Political Economy, Volume 1* he makes the following assertion:

"Within the capitalist system all methods for raising the social productiveness of labour are brought about at the cost of the individual labourer; all means for the development of production transform themselves into means of domination over, and exploitation of, the producers; they mutilate the labourer into a fragment of a man, degrade him to the level of an appendage of a machine, destroy every remnant of charm in his work and

Part 1: Where does our financial system come from?

turn it into a hated toil; they estrange from him the intellectual potentialities of the labour process in the same proportion as science is incorporated in it as an independent power; they distort the conditions under which he works, subject him during the labour process to a despotism the more hateful for its meanness; they transform his life-time into working-time, and drag his wife and child beneath the wheels of the Juggernaut of capital. But all methods for the production of surplus-value are at the same time methods of accumulation; and every extension of accumulation becomes again a means for the development of those methods. It follows therefore that in proportion as capital accumulates, the lot of the labourer, be his payment high or low, must grow worse. The law, finally, that always equilibrates the relative surplus population, or industrial reserve army, to the extent and energy of accumulation, this law rivets the labourer to capital more firmly than the wedges of Vulcan did Prometheus to the rock. It establishes an accumulation of misery, corresponding with accumulation of capital. Accumulation of wealth at one pole is, therefore, at the same time accumulation of misery, agony of toil slavery, ignorance, brutality, mental degradation, at the opposite pole, i.e., on the side of the class that produces its own product in the form of capital."

Marx made a strong statement he predicted that capitalism would inevitably be overthrown by a worker-led class war. This prediction turned out to be somewhat short-sighted, as capitalism still persists today.

Part 1: Where does our financial system come from?

Nonetheless Marx created a whole political movement Marxism.

Karl Marx (1875 portrait by John Jabez Edwin Mayall)

However, one could wonder if we actually live in a truly capitalist system and if a worker-led class war could possibly still happen, which we will speak about later on.

Part 1: Where does our financial system come from?

Marxism highly influenced the Russian Revolution in 1917. Led by the Bolsheviks, the revolution overthrew the Provisional Government and established the world's first socialist state, the Soviet Union, in 1922.

After that, there was an ideological conflict in the world, with one side believing in capitalism and the other not. However, capitalism became the dominant economic system in the world in the 20th century. Capitalism as we know it today was laid in the aftermath of WWII at the Bretton Woods Conference. The Bretton Woods Conference aimed to establish a global trade and finance system for post-war reconstruction. Delegates agreed on a fixed exchange rate system based on the U.S. dollar. They formed the International Monetary Fund (IMF) and the World Bank to oversee financial and trade policies. Globalisation was boosted.

In 1971, U.S. President Richard Nixon made the significant decision to halt the direct international convertibility of the U.S. dollar to gold. This was a significant shift from the Bretton Woods system, which mandated that countries balance their international accounts in dollars that could be converted to gold at a fixed rate of $35 per ounce. However, by the 1960s, the U.S. balance of payments had worsened due to various factors, including the increased competitiveness of exports from Europe and Japan, military expenditures, and foreign aid. This led to an oversupply of dollars globally, and eventually, the amount of dollars held abroad exceeded the U.S. gold reserves. This imbalance exposed the U.S. to the risk of a gold run and eroded confidence in

Part 1: Where does our financial system come from?

the U.S. government's ability to fulfil its obligations. It was the beginning of Fiat currencies. Fiat currency is money whose value, not linked to physical commodities, is based on the issuing government's promise and user's agreed trust in it. At that moment the world became dependant of the dollar and the government institutions issuing it – the Federal Reserve Bank of The United States.

Later, the General Agreement on Tariffs and Trade (GATT) was introduced to promote free trade through reduced tariffs. It is the capitalist system as we know it. In this system and circumstances, stock exchanges, investment firms, mutual funds, and ETFs could be created to enable anyone to profit from their money and create a return for investors. Capitalism triumphed globally after the fall of the Berlin Wall in November 1989.

As we conclude this chapter, it's crucial to acknowledge the unprecedented growth that capitalism has spurred on a global scale in a relatively short span of time. No other system known could have accomplish something similar.

In the year 1500, the world population was approximately 450 million; fast forward to today, and it has skyrocketed to over 8 billion.

Similarly, the world's Gross Domestic Product (GDP) – the total monetary value of all finished goods and services produced worldwide – was around $250 billion in 1500. Today, it has surged to an astounding $105 trillion, a significant leap from the $30 trillion recorded in 2000.

Part 1: Where does our financial system come from?

Capitalism has undeniably catalysed immense growth worldwide, with industries expanding at an accelerated pace. However, it's worth questioning whether capitalism has been an entirely positive force. Is such exponential growth beneficial for us?

One of the inherent issues with capitalism is that profits are not necessarily earned or distributed equitably. A stark example of this is the transatlantic slave trade that occurred from the 17th to the 19th centuries, where slaves were transported to plantations. This historical event serves as a grim reminder that fairness and morality are not always guaranteed under capitalism. Often profits are the main driver.

Part 1: Where does our financial system come from?

Creation of index funds and their evolution

Let's look at some of these institutions that generated massive profits under capitalism. One of those are index funds. A universally utilized industry that remains largely unknown.

First, of all, what is an index fund? Index funds are investment funds that aim to replicate the performance of a specific financial market index. These funds passively track the composition of the chosen index, providing investors with broad market exposure and typically offering a low-cost investment option.

The idea of building a portfolio of different investments to have investments hedging one another appeared in the 1940s. It was a man named Alfred Winslow Jones who created the first hedge fund strategy in 1949. The idea was great. The US economy was booming after the war, so being able to have investments in many different assets or stocks reported much better returns than investing only in one place. Alfred Winslow Jones created the first hedge fund in 1952. It was the first portfolio or investment pool to combine a hedging strategy, leverage, and fees. Then, in the 1960s, numerous new hedge funds emerged after many people had witnessed the performance of the Jones hedge fund.

In the 1960s and early 1970s, MIT professor Paul Cootner made significant contributions to understanding stock market prices in his book *The Random Character of*

Part 1: Where does our financial system come from?

Stock Market Prices. Cootner's research was centred on the "random walk" theory of security pricing. According to this theory, stock prices take a random trajectory, rendering it impossible to forecast future price movements based solely on historical price data. This idea is a key tenet behind index funds, as it suggests that consistently surpassing the market average is improbable, thereby making index funds a practical investment strategy due to their broad market exposure. The research conducted by Cootner, along with the efforts of other scholars in the field, established the foundation for creating and accepting index funds within the investment sector. His work has had a profound and enduring influence on the discipline of financial economics. Within time and results, investors realised it was much safer than investing in individual stocks.

In the 1970s, many hedge funds crashed due to the economic crisis and the spikes in oil prices. Still, the first practical implementation of an index fund was introduced by John C. Bogle who, after being fired by Wellington Fund, decided to found Vanguard, the second largest investment fund in the world today. In 1976, Vanguard created the first index fund, the "Vanguard 500 Index" Fund. The fund was created to track the performance of the S&P 500[19]. The S&P 500 was already launched in

---

[19] The S&P 500 is an index that measures the performance of 500 large companies listed on the stock exchange in the United States.

Part 1: Where does our financial system come from?

1957 by the credit rating agency Standard and Poor's but it was only an index, it wasn't a fund yet. It marked a significant turning point in the history of investing when Vanguard offered such an investment to its client because index funds such as the ones tracking the S&P 500 are considered today, one of the best performing investment through time because of their diversification.

In the 1980s, the changing market offered many opportunities for investment firms. Many funds flourished, making enormous amounts of money, Christopher Leonard says it well: "the largest funds were commanding upwards of $ 1 billion each [...] The combination of an unconstrained investment style, the use of instruments to enhance leverage, and large movements in the currency and commodity markets generated enormous returns for investors on the right side of the trade." The index funds industry growth is impressive. According to an article in the Financial Times in 2021, there are over 16 trillion dollars in assets under management in index funds of various types, almost twice the size of the combined private equity, venture capital and hedge fund industries.

As John Coates observes in his book *The Problem of Twelve* (I will often mention him since he has made some great observations on the topic of index funds and private equity), "The Bottom line is that index funds now own

Part 1: Where does our financial system come from?

more than 20 percent of large US public companies. If current growth rates continued indefinitely, the entire US market would be held by such funds by 2035. [...] But even if the trend flattens, the majority of many public companies will soon be owned by index funds." Coates observes "that even if this mega-trend begins to taper off, the majority of the thousand largest US companies could be controlled by a dozen or fewer people over the next ten to twenty years." Isn't it scary? However, that's not the only problem.

Imagine standing on the edge of a vast spider web, intricately woven and stretching as far as the eye can see. This web represents our financial system, and each thread symbolizes the ties between a select group of individuals who hold the reins of most industries.

These individuals are not isolated islands; they are more like nodes in a network, each owning stakes in the others' ventures. This forms a tightly-knit, interconnected system, much like the threads of the spider web.

Now, picture a single thread snapping. The entire web vibrates, the ripples spreading outwards, affecting every other thread. This is the profound implication of our interconnected system: should one node falter, the ripple effects could potentially destabilize the entire system, impacting us all.

We will delve deeper into this network in the next chapter.

The interconnectedness of our financial system

When you look at the different shareholders of the biggest banks, investment firms or companies, you often see the same names multiple times. For example, BlackRock's biggest shareholder is Vanguard and Vanguard's biggest shareholder is BlackRock. What does this mean?

An interconnected banking system – each bank has exposure in other banks – as we have today is not always a bad thing, as it allows banks to obtain funding or transfer risk. However, it is not good for the stability of the financial system. The more that banks are interconnected, the higher the risk of panic spreading through them. In the same way that greater proximity between humans increases the speed of virus contagion and distance slows it down, so interconnectedness is a key determinant to understanding how fast a crisis will spread and how bad it can become.

As Nassim Nicholas Taleb, a famous statistician dealing with uncertainty, wrote in his book *The Black Swan*: "We have moved from a diversified ecology of small banks, with varied lending policies, to a more homogeneous framework of firms that all resemble one another. True, we now have fewer failures, but when they occur... I shiver at the thought. I rephrase here: we will have fewer but more severe crises. The rarer the event, the less we know about its odds. It means that we know less and less about the possibility of a crisis."

Future crisis will be unpredictable and will have disastrous consequences.

First, there is direct interconnectedness. Banks issue loans to each other all the time. They hold each other's securities, they have derivatives with each other such as futures contracts or options, and they exchange securities financing transactions that are loans with bonds or shares as collateral. If Bank A lends money to Bank B in the interbank market, the two banks are directly connected. If one bank fails, others will be directly affected.

On the other hand, there is indirect interconnectedness, it refers to the interconnectedness that arises from shared exposure. Banks own assets, so if a bank wants to sell a particular asset, it will indirectly affect the bank owning that asset. If two banks have significant exposure to the same sector of the economy, they are indirectly interconnected. If that sector experiences a downturn, both banks would be affected, even though there are no clear direct financial relations between them.

Confidence is a significant example of indirect interconnectedness. If one bank fails, the confidence in other similar banks is affected, too. Often, investors will withdraw their money after losing confidence in the banking system, resulting in liquidity shortages for other banks.

When there is a crisis, both direct and indirect interconnectedness play a role. For example, Lehman Brothers, like many financial institutions, relied heavily on short-term funding, including repurchase agreements[20] (repo loans), to finance its operations and investments before the 2008 financial crisis. Repo loans involve borrowing money by pledging securities as collateral, with an agreement to repurchase them at a later date. With diminishing confidence in Lehman Brothers, its access to the repo markets became restricted. Other financial institutions, concerned about the quality of Lehman's collateral, were less willing to lend to the company through repo agreements. The reduced access to repo markets meant Lehman had trouble rolling over its short-term debt and obtaining the necessary funding to maintain its operations. It led to a severe liquidity crisis, making it difficult for Lehman to cover its maturing debts and meet its financial obligations. Finally, this led the firm to bankruptcy. Almost no bank can sustain a bank run because banks do not have enough capital on hand to be self-sufficient as we have seen in previous chapters.

---

[20] A short-term financial transaction where one party sells securities to another with an agreement to repurchase them at an agreed-upon date and price. These transactions involve collateral, typically government securities or other high-quality assets, serving as security for the loan. The party selling the securities (the borrower) receives cash, and the party buying the securities (the lender) earns interest on the cash until the borrower repurchases the securities. Repo loans are commonly used in financial markets for short-term funding and liquidity management.

In the example of Lehman, Lehman needed these repo loans to survive, and a drop in investor confidence was enough for Lehman Brothers to fail.
This drop of confidence among investors was evident during the financial crisis, with Bear Stearns, followed by Lehman Brothers, and subsequently, AIG (American International Group). This cycle perpetuates until measures are taken to halt the liquidity shortages and restore confidence.

Index funds are also highly interconnected. The interconnectedness of index funds arises from their diversified and weighted investments in various companies across different countries and their susceptibility to global economic events and cycles. This interconnectedness is a double-edged sword: it can lead to higher returns when the market is doing well, but it can also lead to larger losses during market downturns. So far, the index funds industry has found itself in a very profitable position.

We are speaking about entities such as banks, but due to the rise in globalisation during the last decade, our economy is much more interconnected. Countries are highly interconnected too. The financial crisis in 2008 hit Europe and many other regions of the world too. The next crisis will be felt everywhere on the planet.

In conclusion, the interconnectedness of our global financial system, while offering benefits such as risk diversification and expanded investment opportunities, also presents a significant challenge. As noted by the

International Monetary Fund, the difficulty of the issue lies in effectively managing these risks while simultaneously reaping their benefits. But herein lies the conundrum: how can we ensure that these risks are being managed appropriately? Especially when the primary objective of financial institutions is to maximize profit, a goal that doesn't always align with the broader good.

As we transition into the next section of this book, we will delve deeper into the implications of this environment. We will explore how the very interconnectedness and capitalistic nature of our financial system have inadvertently led to a concentration of wealth and a system where all entities are intricately linked. This exploration will shed light on the complexities of our financial system and the challenges we face in ensuring its stability and fairness.

Part 2:

How does this environment lead to an economy where all entities are connected to each other, and one entity has control over a part of all of them?

Part 2: Causes of wealth and power concentration

How did capitalism, free markets, and private central banking lead to a concentration of wealth and power in the hands of a few entities?

Capitalism, free markets, and private central banking are fundamental components of many modern economies. While they have contributed to significant economic growth and prosperity, they have also been associated with a rise in wealth concentration.

The cornerstone of capitalism is the profit motive. Businesses strive to maximise profits, which often leads to wealth accumulation. Successful entities can reinvest their profits to generate even more income, creating a cycle of wealth accumulation. Over time, this can result in a small number of entities controlling a significant portion of the economy's wealth, as we will soon see. It should not be forgotten that capitalism is characterised by the right to own private property. This includes both tangible assets, such as real estate, and intangible assets, such as stocks and bonds. Entities that can acquire and control a large amount of these assets can amass substantial wealth. Ownership of these assets generates income, further contributing to wealth concentration.

Capitalism based on a "free market" and the idea of equilibrium between supply and demand, gives opportunities to entities with significant resources to potentially manipulate these points of equilibrium to their advantage. But is capitalism an actual "free market"? Firms are political entities that aim to maximise profits amidst uncertainty, which requires planning. They have the autonomy to decide on pricing, worker compensation, investment, innovation, advertising, and lobbying. They can decide how they wish to be run. Therefore, bigger firms have more market power and, hence, more planning power. The decisions of large multinational corporation's impact society at large, influencing innovation and politics. The state should be a neutral entity maintaining a "free market", making sure that competition exists, and monopolies do not arise. This is, however, not the case. The state is, like any other entity, also influenced by societal power relations, such as social norms, politics, and how our society is organised. Once this is understood, it is hard to believe that capitalist markets are "free". Conversely, this "free" market created an environment where a few entities have much more power than others.

For example, owning stock of a company gives you the right to participate in shareholders' votes, enabling the approval or disapproval of how the company is run, or even asking the company to be run differently. The biggest shareholder, or a few entities, have the possibility to influence companies to act in their best interests. This gives bigger entities more influencing power.

Lastly, private central banking is a direct concentration of wealth. In most capitalist economies, central banks are privately owned. These banks can control the money supply, which is a clear concentration of financial power in a few hands. By influencing interest rates and lending

Part 2: Causes of wealth and power concentration

practices, private central banks can significantly impact the distribution of wealth within an economy. The largest shareholders of private banks, as Mayer Amschel Rothschild ironically said, have control of the money supply and thus control of the country.

Private central banking facilitates the accessibility of easy money for entities with privileged access, enabling them to amass wealth and enhance their financial positions. Big investment firms have taken this to their advantage.

In a Tribune article written by Grace Blakeley, entitled "How Capitalism Concentrates Power", she mentions: "Capitalism is a system built upon the domination of labour by capital". She adds to it a pertinent explanation: "Our economy is not governed by the principles of perfect competition you might see in a textbook, but neither is it centrally planned. Instead, we live under a form of oligarchic capitalism in which a number of very powerful agents are able to shape the system to promote their own power and wealth. [...] As capitalism has become more concentrated and centralised, the decisions taken by key actors within firms have become far more important in shaping the development of the system. Monopolistic and oligopolistic corporations have a huge command over our collective resources, and what they decide to do with those resources impacts every-one. Firms have political power, but no accountability — and in that sense we can speak of oligopolistic planning, counterposed to democratic and socialised planning."

Part 2: Causes of wealth and power concentration

This is the problem we face in most of the world today: a few entities control most of the market.

Blakely argues that firms lack accountability, implying that their decisions can impact everyone in society, but there is no effective mechanism to hold them responsible for the consequences of their actions. This lack of accountability is seen as a significant issue, particularly in contrast to the principles of democratic and socialised planning. The term "oligopolistic planning" describes the decision-making power of a few powerful entities in shaping the economic system. This is contrasted with the idea of "democratic and socialised planning," which suggests a more inclusive and accountable decision-making process that involves a broader representation of the population. Through democratic planning, instead of a small group of individuals or corporations making crucial decisions, a broader representation of the population, possibly through democratic institutions, plays a role in shaping economic policies. Socialised planning goes a step further by emphasising collective or social ownership of key industries and means of production.

While capitalism, free markets, and private central banking lead to wealth concentration, they also have mechanisms such as competition and the freedom to choose, which can act as counterbalances. The extent to which wealth concentration occurs can vary greatly depending on the specific form of capitalism in place. Therefore, while these systems can create an environment conducive to wealth concentration, they do not inevitably

Part 2: Causes of wealth and power concentration

lead to this outcome. It is the responsibility of governments and societies to try not to be influenced by these big entities, if possible, or at least to implement checks and balances to ensure a fair distribution of wealth and prevent the undue concentration of economic power. The problem is that in most countries, this is not the case. Governments have lost control over their money supplies and don't regulate the financial markets correctly. Without sufficient regulation, entities with more resources can exploit the system to their advantage. While it is surely no easy task to regulate our economy and financial markets correctly, a necessary first step is to acknowledge the growing concentration of wealth and power in the hands of a few and recognise that this is a huge problem.

Later, I will detail an example of massive wealth concentration: BlackRock.

Part 2: Causes of wealth and power concentration

Financial stability

As seen earlier, the interconnectedness of financial institutions poses a significant risk to the stability of the financial system. When a single institution encounters a substantial problem, the repercussions can quickly spread throughout the system, culminating in a financial crisis. The 2008 global financial crisis serves as a stark illustration of the perils associated with interconnectedness, where issues originating in the subprime mortgage market triggered a domino effect, impacting banks and financial institutions worldwide.

In addition to the challenges of interconnectedness, banks contribute to economic dynamics through the fractional reserve banking system. Within this system, banks are required to reserve only a fraction of deposits, enabling them to lend out the remaining funds. While this facilitates a short-term expansion of the money supply, it can have lasting effects. In the longer term, it often leads to asset price inflation, benefiting wealthier individuals who hold a substantial portion of their assets in these inflated markets. Consequently, wealth concentration and income inequality tend to increase.

The creation of money "out of nothing" by banks comes with the burden of interest rates that must be repaid. Over time, this can impede economic growth and widen the wealth gap. The ability of banks to generate money "out of nothing" contributes to the accumulation of debt in the economy. Excessive levels of debt pose a threat to financial stability and can precipitate economic downturns. The availability of easy credit further fuels the risk of asset bubbles, such as those seen in real estate or stock markets, which, when they burst, can lead to severe financial crises.

Similarly, the benefits of economic growth resulting from banks creating money through lending tend to favour those with access to credit. This exacerbates income inequality, as wealthier individuals and corporations with better credit access are positioned to invest and accumulate more wealth.

The inherent challenge in a fractional reserve system lies in the fact that banks have the authority to generate money through the process of extending loans, which leads to the creation of additional money through subsequent loans built upon the foundation of the initial ones, again and again. It is like putting gasoline on a fire, with the burden of substantial debt, the system perpetually is on the brink of collapsing. If these loans lead to financial instability and crises, governments may be compelled to bail out the banking system to prevent a broader economic collapse. This happened in 2008 when the Fed bailed out AIG with the result that taxpayer money was being used to support financial institutions, effectively transferring wealth from the general population to the banking sector.

In summary, the interconnected financial system, coupled with the practices of fractional reserve banking, present a complex web of challenges that can contribute to systemic risks, economic imbalances, and increased wealth

Part 2: Causes of wealth and power concentration

concentration over time. Alternatives, such as state banking and the gold standard, can be more restrictive. State banks are often subject to more regulations and may not offer the same range of services as private banks. However, state banks can provide quite a few benefits to their peoples, such as money without interest for their governments and a low risk of default. The gold standard, which ties the value of a currency to a specific amount of gold, can limit the amount of money that can be created and thus restrict liquidity. If too much money is issued in both systems, devaluations in respect of other currencies will happen. It is difficult to find the right system where capitalism works at its best without concentrating wealth in the hands of a few and not creating risks for taxpayers. Addressing these issues involves a combination of monetary policy, banking regulation, and broader economic policies aimed at promoting a more inclusive and equitable distribution of wealth. We must find a balance between promoting economic growth and safeguarding against systemic risks. However, it is important to recognise that fractional reserve banking and interconnectedness are just one terrible aspect of a complex economic system, and that other factors can also contribute to wealth concentration.

Let's delve into the amassed wealth of one such entity, BlackRock, and explore the strategies and decisions that led to its remarkable financial growth.

Part 2: Causes of wealth and power concentration

How one entity could acquire so much wealth: the rise of BlackRock

We have spoken about the economic environment we are in, where rich entities become even richer amassing a substantial amount of wealth in an interconnected financial system. Wealth concentration by a few entities is recurrent. We have discussed capitalism as the system we operate in. As Larry Fink says: "Capitalism has the power to shape society and act as a powerful catalyst for change." Let's see how BlackRock shaped our society.

First of all, how did BlackRock, the world's largest investment company to date, succeed in becoming so influential?

BlackRock was founded in 1988 as a risk-management firm for its clients. It began as part of the Blackstone Group, a private equity firm, and was initially called Blackstone Financial Management. In 1992, BlackRock became an independent company, and its name was changed to BlackRock, Inc. During the late 1990s, BlackRock expanded its investment management capabilities and offerings across various asset classes, including fixed income, equities, and alternatives. BlackRock launched its IPO (Initial Public Offering) on the New York Stock Exchange on the first of October 1999. Its share price was $14 per share, and by the end of 1999, the firm made $165 billion in AUM. Today, its share price sits close to $800 with a peak of $950 in 2021.

Part 2: Causes of wealth and power concentration

The company focused on risk management and analytics, leveraging technology to enhance its investment strategies. It expanded its business rapidly through strategic acquisitions, including the acquisition of State Street Research & Management in 2005, the purchase of Merrill Lynch Investment Management, and the purchase of Barclays Global Investors in 2009 after the financial crisis. The purchase significantly increased its assets under management. BlackRock's success is mainly attributed to its disciplined investment strategies, its global presence, and its extensive use of technology and data analytics.

BlackRock started proposing ETFs to its clients very early in 1995, but it wasn't very successful until 2009 when it bought iShares from Barclays Global Investors. iShares were key to the success of BlackRock. Buying Barclays Global Investors in 2009 gave it access to a prominent industry, the index funds industry. It quickly became a major player in the ETF market, and its revolutionary iShares ETFs have become some of the most widely traded and recognised ETFs globally. BlackRock launched iShares Core in 2012. BlackRock explains in its report "Introducing iShares and ETFs" in 2015: "An iShares ETF combines the diversification benefits of an index mutual fund with the trading convenience of a share. iShares funds are traded on-exchange, and the funds aim to match the performance of a specified market index." The ETF market represented 5.75 trillion of assets under management in 2019. Some predictions suggest ETFs

Part 2: Causes of wealth and power concentration

globally could hit 30 trillion dollars in AUM by 2033. The largest part of the ETFs industry is the equities or stock ETFs such as the S&P 500. In August 2019, the index fund industry reached a milestone when the $4.27 trillion in passively managed U.S. stock funds outflanked the $4.25 trillion run by stockpickers[21]. BlackRock is the main and biggest player in this market.

Today, BlackRock is the largest ETF provider with close to 2,5 trillion of total assets under management in ETFs. Recently, in June 2023, BlackRock started to get involved in cryptocurrencie, wanting to create an iShare Bitcoin spot ETF, but it did not receive clearance from the SEC which ruled that BlackRock had not shown it could protect investors from market manipulations. However, at the beginning of 2024, on January 10th, the SEC finally approved it, and BlackRock launched one of the first cryptocurrency ETFs, IBIT. Once again, BlackRock is leading the industry, taking action on future technologies that could become very prominent. According to an article of TheBitTimes on CoinMarketCap, "Spot Bitcoin ETFs (exchange-traded funds) generated $1.8 billion in volume on Jan. 16, three times more than the combined trading

---

[21] Stockpickers are individuals or professionals who select and invest in specific individual stocks or securities based on their analysis and strategies, with the goal of outperforming the broader market.

volume that same day for all 500 ETFs that were launched in the US in 2023."

BlackRock's ability to capitalise on these developments is what has made it so successful today. Another example is in 2018, when it was already investing in AI. BlackRock had established its premier AI Lab in Palo Alto with the objective of accelerating the integration of artificial intelligence and its subfields, such as machine learning, data science, and natural language processing. This step may have optimised results and stimulated growth for the company, its clients, and investors.

However, BlackRock's success is not only due to its strong presence in the ETFs market. Its advisory business, known as BlackRock Solutions, was founded in the year 2000. This marked the beginning of BlackRock's role as a technology provider. The basis for this business was and still is Aladdin, BlackRock's proprietary technology. This technology is integral to who they are as a firm and is embedded in everything they do. It differentiates them as an investment and risk manager. Aladdin is an acronym for Asset, Liability and Debt, Derivative Investment Network. According to TGH Editorial Team, it is "executing trades in every asset class. Aladdin controls approximately more than half of ETFs, 10% of the stock market and 17% of the bond market. Aladdin is a vast network of around 5000 supercomputers that work together to act as the central nervous system for investors and asset managers across the globe." It executes an average of 250,000 trades per day. Aladdin had more than 21 trillion AUM in 2020. A report from the Financial

Part 2: Causes of wealth and power concentration

Times found around $21.6 trillion in assets sitting on the platform from just a third of its 240 clients. We don't know exactly how much it is today since BlackRock no longer reports that number, possibly because it could scare some people or attract too much attention. The same Financial Times article says: "Vanguard and State Street Global Advisors, the largest fund managers after BlackRock, are users, as are half the top 10 insurers by assets, as well as Japan's $1.5tn government pension fund, the world's largest. Apple, Microsoft, and Google's parent firm, Alphabet — the three biggest US public companies — all rely on the system to steward hundreds of billions of dollars in their corporate treasury investment portfolios." Aladdin manages the money of the most important countries and companies worldwide. It is BlackRock's secret tool. A significant part of BlackRock's success can be attributed to Aladdin's success.

While BlackRock is classified as an investment firm it also provides an advisory business to some of its clients. The most important is its "Financial Markets Advisory" (FMA), a division of BlackRock, which was founded amidst the financial crisis in April 2008. Its primary role, as BlackRock describes it, is to provide dedicated assistance to various entities such as governments, central banks, and global financial institutions. It provides a comprehensive array of services to both public and private sector institutions. It capitalises on BlackRock's robust data and risk analytics, advanced technology, and financial modelling expertise. Simultaneously, it upholds strict information barriers and implements rigorous procedures to prevent and manage any potential conflicts of interest. We can believe that it uses Aladdin for its advisory business too. As we will soon see, conflicts of interest exist even though BlackRock claims to have "stringent information barriers".

Strategically, BlackRock has hired many important former government officials in senior roles inside the company, such as the senior advisor to President Barack Obama and Stanley Fischer, a former U.S. Federal Reserve Vice Chair. BlackRock has not only recruited strategic people in the US. In the UK, it hired George Osborne, former Chancellor of the Exchequer. He implemented pension reform and gave BlackRock access to a £25 billion market. In Germany, it is Friedrich Merz, former head of Angela Merkel's party (CDU), who currently manages the local operations of the asset manager. In Switzerland, Philippe Hildebrand, the former head of the Swiss Central Bank, was recruited. In Greece, BlackRock has opted for Paschalis Bouchoris, the former head of a government privatisation programme. BlackRock has recruited vital figures, each having essential experience that significantly benefit the firm.

BlackRock was one of the first firms to start emphasising environmental, social, and governance (ESG) factors in its investment decisions and promote it through its governance and shareholder votes. It is trying to find more sustainable investments (investments that are ranked with a high ESG), making the firm more attractive to new investors, and collecting new fees from investors.

Recently, BlackRock acquired Global Infrastructure Partners, making a 12.5 billion dollar bet on the infrastructure market. The deal is expected to close in Q3 of 2024. The company has commented that long-term structural societal changes such as decarbonisation will favour investment in infrastructure in both the coming years and decades.

Part 2: Causes of wealth and power concentration

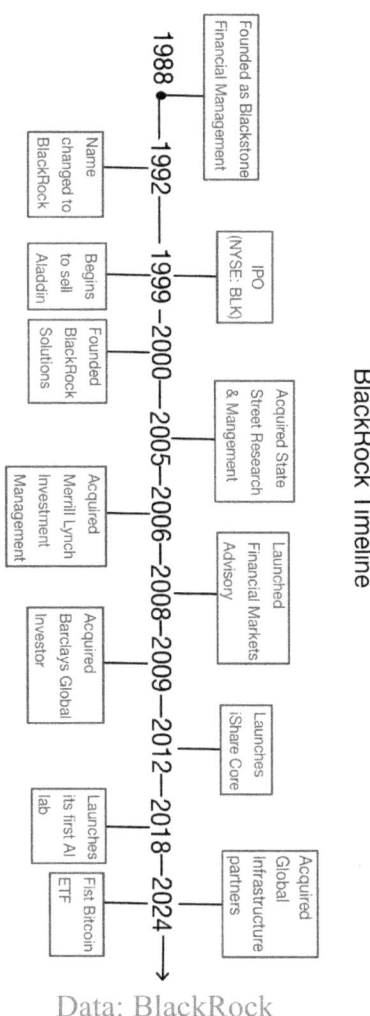

Data: BlackRock

Part 2: Causes of wealth and power concentration

In the following graph, we can see the impressive growth of BlackRock's assets since the financial crisis.

Total assets under management (AUM) of BlackRock from 2008 to 2023.

Part 2: Causes of wealth and power concentration

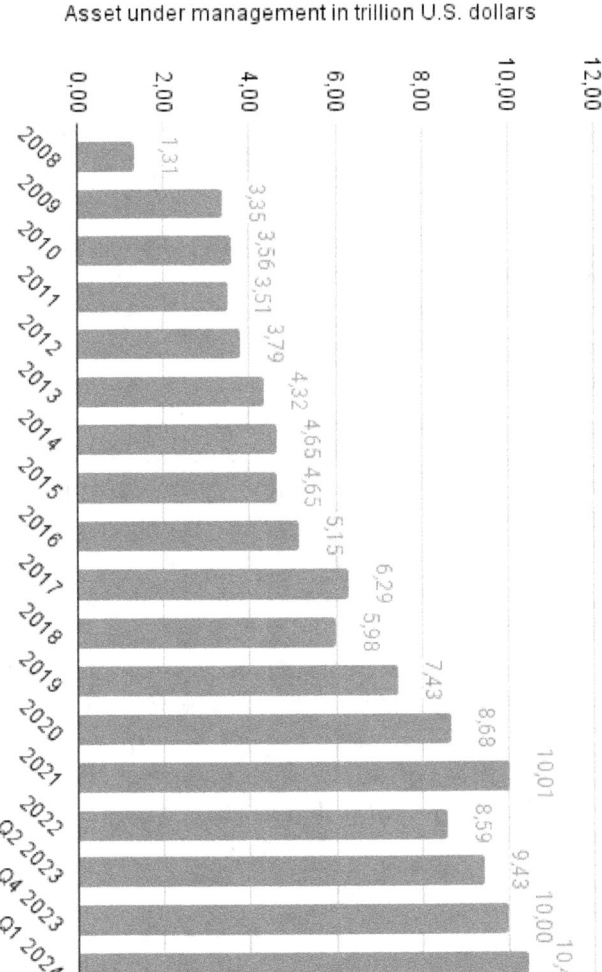

Data: BlackRock

Part 2: Causes of wealth and power concentration

BlackRock's past actions and influence

Now that we know how BlackRock became the most important company of the 21st century, let's get into the field and look at clear examples from the past where BlackRock has played an important role in situations where its influence cannot be denied. During economic downturns and crisis, governments have often turned to BlackRock because of BlackRock's risk management algorithm, Aladdin. It also took part in some politically important investments.

While Vanguard, BlackRock's biggest competitor, mainly focuses on indexed strategies, BlackRock, State Street, and Fidelity (the 4 biggest investment firms by AUM) also manage large active funds, which augment the governance power they wield by also being large index fund advisors. Some of the examples that follow will confirm this.

It is important to note that these are only a few pertinent examples of what I found online. There is much more to be discovered. The biggest part is undisclosed to the public and any official data understates the actual problem. Therefore, what I will show you is only the tip of the iceberg.

Part 2: Causes of wealth and power concentration

The 2008 financial crisis

To begin with, BlackRock played a critical role during the 2008 financial crisis. Many banks turned to BlackRock for advice or even sold some of their bad debt to BlackRock.

The Federal Reserve and the Treasury Department granted contracts to BlackRock for the management of $130 billion in bad debt that had previously been held by Bear Stearns and American International Group Inc. (AIG). Both Bear Stearns and AIG faced significant financial difficulties in the aftermath of the 2008 financial crisis. Bear Stearns experienced a liquidity crisis and was ultimately acquired by JPMorgan Chase in March 2008 to prevent its bankruptcy. AIG also faced severe financial problems and received a bailout from the U.S. government to prevent its bankruptcy in September 2008. They were both on the brink of collapse and required intervention to avoid financial catastrophe.

Matthew Goldstein, an NYT journalist, wrote: "The firm helped price and sell those assets for the government at the same time it was helping private clients buy similar assets." On one hand, BlackRock was contracted by the Federal Reserve and the Treasury Department to manage distressed assets and assist in the sale of these assets for the government, which can be seen as a public interest role. On the other hand, BlackRock also assisted private clients in purchasing similar distressed assets, a for-profit activity. This dual role raised questions about conflicts of interest. Did BlackRock have an advantage in the private market due to its involvement with government assets?

Part 2: Causes of wealth and power concentration

"How is it that only one company is qualified to manage these assets recovered by the government?" asked Republican Senator Charles Grassley.

BlackRock was also one of four co-managers of a $500 billion Fed program, which had been announced in November 2008 and expanded to $1.25 trillion in March 2009, for the purchase of residential mortgage-backed securities.

The Fed has not made public the contract it signed with BlackRock. It had planned to share information about it, but even today, more than ten years after the crisis, the full details of the firm's earnings have not been disclosed.

In addition, there is the Fed program, quantitative easing (QE), where the Fed buys a range of financial assets, such as bonds or stocks, to pump the economy with new money that started after the crisis. Todd Rosenbluth, the head of E.T.F. and mutual fund research for CFRA, a research firm, said that BlackRock dominated the market for the kinds of bonds and ETFs the Fed said it would buy. BlackRock was very well positioned. We can see in the AUM graph illustrated earlier between 2008 and 2009, BlackRock's AUM more than doubled. This is mainly due to the acquisition of Barclays Global Investors. However, BlackRock was one of the few firms to be able to make money through the crisis. When taxpayers had to pay for the greedy actions of the biggest banks, BlackRock was well positioned in the market and ready to give advices that would highly benefit its previous investments. BlackRock was the go-to bank for help during the crash.

Part 2: Causes of wealth and power concentration

An adviser for central banks

Similarly, BlackRock has been an adviser for central banks of different countries.

In 2011, the Central Bank of Ireland contacted BlackRock to evaluate the state of the six main Irish banks. Three of them had just been bailed out in a panic by the state to avoid bankruptcy. The finance minister's decision to engage BlackRock was driven by pressure from international institutions that had provided loans to Ireland. These international institutions were collectively called the "Troika" and were known for their involvement in managing the eurozone crisis. The Troika consisted of three key entities: the European Central Bank (ECB), the European Union (EU), and the International Monetary Fund (IMF). How is it that international institutions push a country to engage a giant that has investments all over the country such as BlackRock?

Then, in Greece in 2011, also under pressure from the Troika, the Central Bank of Greece called on BlackRock to look at the loan portfolios of 18 banks, and again in 2013 for the four largest banks. Why did the Troika pressure the central banks to contact BlackRock in both cases and not another firm? Again, does BlackRock have a business relationship with the ECB, the EU and the IMF?

In Spain, four of the largest real estate developers have BlackRock among their investors, as do the six largest Spanish banks. However, in May 2012, the government asked BlackRock to evaluate the bad debts and real estate

Part 2: Causes of wealth and power concentration

assets of the country's credit institutions, along with determining their requirements for recapitalisation. BlackRock was on both sides of the job again.

Then, in the Netherlands, in December 2012, the central bank requested that BlackRock examine the loan portfolio of ING, the national banking giant. Additionally, in July 2013, they were tasked with assessing the real estate assets of all Dutch banks. It's worth noting that BlackRock already had a stake of more than 5% in ING across approximately twenty sectors.

When questioned by a Member of Parliament, Finance Minister Jeroen Dijsselbloem, who concurrently held the position of President of the Eurogroup at that time, defended his actions by pointing to the presence of a "Chinese wall" separating BlackRock's advisory and fund management operations.

Paradoxically, the Dutch central bank had decided in 2007 to assign the responsibility of managing its employee's pension funds to BlackRock. Is there no conflict of interest?

BlackRock's advisory business worked constantly with central banks of different countries to analyse portfolios or debt of companies and banks. Simultaneously, Blackrock's fund business had been investing in the same companies and banks in these countries.

Part 2: Causes of wealth and power concentration

The pandemic

At the onset of the 2020 pandemic, the Federal Reserve turned to BlackRock for assistance in navigating the financial crisis. The CEO of BlackRock, Mr. Fink, maintained frequent communication with Mr. Mnuchin, head of treasury and Mr. Powell, chairman of the Fed, in the critical days before and after the Fed's announcement of the emergency rescue programmes in late March.

In collaboration with the US government, Mr. Fink played an important role in devising various components of the financial rescue plan, evident through email conversations. One aspect of this rescue plan was the decision to purchase corporate bonds, which included both the debt that already existed and new bonds that were being issued. In simpler terms, the government was investing in these bonds to provide financial support to struggling companies.

Again, BlackRock extended its support to the government by executing the programme at a reduced cost. It waived fees associated with purchasing exchange-traded funds and rebated fees from its own iShares ETFs to the New York Fed. This gesture by BlackRock reduced the overall expenses of the rescue plan. It demonstrated its commitment to supporting the government's efforts to stabilise the financial markets and assist businesses during challenging times.

This time, the terms of the agreement were clear in contrast to the one in 2008. It is important to note that BlackRock benefited substantially from this rescue package, as it was actively selling bonds and ETFs. The programme had to work properly in the interest of BlackRock.

Mr. Fink's involvement in an evening call at 7:25, along with Mr. Mnuchin, Mr. Powell, and Larry Kudlow, the White House National Economic Council director, just before the significant Fed announcement, as documented in Mr. Mnuchin's calendars, shows how closely Mr. Fink worked with the Fed and the government. It also underscores how the Fed and the government needed the help of BlackRock. It was essential to the success of the rescue package and in stabilising the economy.

The FDIC

It is important to note that the FDIC had officially brought on BlackRock among its contractors for strategic financial advice and consulting work on bank failures as of May 2022. It is important to mention that BlackRock is the second largest investor in US Banks after Vanguard.

The war in Ukraine

Lately, because of the war taking place in the Ukraine, BlackRock and JPMorgan have been having discussions with the Ukraine government to set up a reconstruction bank at the end of hostilities.

The Kyiv government engaged BlackRock's consulting business in November 2022 to determine how to attract enough capital to rebuild Ukraine after the war.

Part 2: Causes of wealth and power concentration

BlackRock is offering their services knowing that its work will give them a preliminary opportunity to explore potential investments within the nation before other financial institutions.

Ukraine needs "a development finance bank to find investment opportunities in sectors such as infrastructure, climate and agriculture and make them attractive to pension funds and other long-term investors and lenders." BlackRock advised.

Constructing that bank will give a very precious edge to BlackRock, knowing that Ukraine is a leader in agriculture, supplying oilseeds and grains to the global market.

At the Ukrainian Infrastructure Forum in London in December 2022, the Deputy Minister of the Ukraine Economy, Oleksandr Gryban, said that Ukraine "will become one of the best in the world in terms of opportunities for investors" after the war.

It is impressive to see how, even before the war has ended, that BlackRock is already having active discussions with the Ukrainian government.

Part 2: Causes of wealth and power concentration

Ukrainian President Volodymyr Zelensky, in a conference call with BlackRock's CEO Larry Fink.

Source: www.president.gov.ua

Investments in China

Furthermore, BlackRock is investing heavily in China. Some of its investments even help the Chinese military, which goes against U.S principles. However, the Biden administration signed an executive order limiting US investments in China in key technology industries in August 2023. The lawmakers expected stricter regulation from Biden. US Representative and Chairman of the House Select Committee on China, Mike Gallagher, said:

"If we want to stop American money funding military contractors and human rights abusers in the PRC [People's Republic of China], then Congress needs to step up and wrestle with this much bigger problem."

According to the House Select Committee on China, BlackRock is reported to have five funds that collectively hold investments exceeding $429 million in Chinese companies that are perceived to be acting contrary to US interests. These funds have holdings in a combined total of 20 companies that are associated with one or more government watch lists, posing a national security risk. BlackRock continue to have these investments to this date without any repercussions.

Failure of Signature and Silicon Valley banks

At the beginning of March 2023, US regulators enlisted BlackRock's assistance in selling a $114 billion portfolio of securities acquired from troubled lenders Signature Bank and Silicon Valley Bank, reinstating once more BlackRock's role as a government advisor during financial crises.

BlackRock oversaw the sale of $27 billion in securities from Signature Bank and $87 billion from Silicon Valley Bank, as stated by the Federal Deposit Insurance Corp. These holdings primarily consisted of various mortgage-related securities and loans that had remained after the government sold the rest of the banks' assets in March 2023.

Part 2: Causes of wealth and power concentration

In the Middle East

BlackRock and Saudi Arabia's sovereign wealth fund[22], the Public Investment Fund (PIF), have signed an agreement to jointly explore infrastructure projects in the Middle East. The PIF aims to grow its assets under management to more than $1 trillion by 2025. Therefore, BlackRock manages the money of one of the most influential states in the Gulf. Saudi Arabia is the world's largest oil supplier, possessing about 18% of the world's proven reserves. BlackRock is advising Saudi Arabia on how to create new value for its economy other than oil for the future. This agreement with Saudi Arabia will be and already is key to a transition to renewable energies worldwide. It will enable BlackRock to have an influence on future decisions and planning in Saudi Arabia and the Middle East.

Nonetheless, BlackRock also wants to create a new fund in the Middle East to allow international investors to invest in the region and boost foreign investments into Saudi Arabia to add value to the Saudi Arabian economy. It is targeting an initial $1 billion fundraising from some of the Middle East's largest sovereign wealth funds for

---

[22] A sovereign wealth fund is a state-owned investment fund that manages and invests a country's reserves, typically derived from revenues such as those from commodity exports or foreign exchange reserves. The purpose is to generate long-term wealth and financial stability for the country.

Part 2: Causes of wealth and power concentration

this new private equity fund focused on infrastructure investments in the Middle East.

However, a potential conflict of interest arises from BlackRock's dual objectives. On one hand, it is an adviser, advising Saudi Arabia on economic diversification and renewable energy transition, aligning with global sustainability goals. On the other hand, BlackRock is an investor, seeking to create a new fund in the Middle East, targeting international investors and aiming to boost foreign investments in Saudi Arabia. This situation could lead to conflicts where BlackRock's advice to Saudi Arabia may be influenced by its own financial interests in the region, potentially compromising the objectivity and effectiveness of its advisory role. Similarly, BlackRock's investment decisions in the region could be influenced by its advisory relationship with Saudi Arabia, potentially prioritizing investments that align with its advisory activities rather than purely financial considerations.

Very recently, BlackRock has come under scrutiny in the context of the Israel-Palestine conflict due to its investments in companies directly or indirectly implicated in Israel's military campaign. Among these companies are Lockheed Martin, Boeing, and Raytheon, which are known for supplying weapons and missiles to Israel. BlackRock owns close to 7% of Lockheed Martin as of February 2023.

While these investments link BlackRock to the region, it does not necessarily imply direct involvement in the conflicts. The ethical implications of such investments are a topic of ongoing debate.

Source: X formally Twitter, @Israel_MOD

In Africa

The UN affirms that Africa's debt reached 1.8 trillion dollars in 2022, a 183% increase since 2010, roughly four times higher than its GDP growth rate in dollar terms. In recent years, private investors, primarily investment funds and pension funds, have emerged as the primary creditors to African nations. As of 2022, they accounted for 42

Part 2: Causes of wealth and power concentration

percent of African foreign public debt, surpassing multilateral institutions like the IMF and World Bank, which held 38 percent, and other nations, which held 20 percent.

BlackRock is currently the largest known bondholder in Zambia, holding $220 million of Zambian bonds, which accounts for 7% of the total bonds. Despite being the largest holder, BlackRock declined Zambia's request to suspend debt payments in 2020 and has not proposed any debt restructuring. The majority of BlackRock's bonds in Zambia were likely acquired after September 2020, indicating a period when Zambia faced challenges meeting its payment obligations.

BlackRock's potential profitability in this situation arises from purchasing bonds below their face value[23] and benefiting from the associated high-interest rates. Since the beginning of the pandemic in early 2020, Zambia's bonds have, on average, been valued at 59 cents on the dollar, with an average interest rate of 8.1%. To explain this more clearly, BlackRock benefits from Zambia's bonds trading below face value as it allows the investment firm to purchase the bonds at a discount, potentially

---

[23] The face value of a bond, also known as its par value or nominal value, is the predetermined amount that the bond issuer agrees to repay to the bondholder at the bond's maturity. It is the amount on which interest payments are calculated, and it represents the principal amount of the bond.

gaining profits when they are repaid at their full-face value. This discounted acquisition also results in higher yields for BlackRock (bond yields are inversely related to their prices). However, for Zambia, the lower trading value indicates increased debt burden and borrowing costs (Zambia is effectively repaying a higher amount in interest compared to the initial proceeds received from the bond issuance). This signals financial challenges and a higher perceived risk of default for Zambia. The elevated interest rates and the trading of the debt at values significantly below face value reflect the considerable risk associated with the possibility of non-repayment. However, for an asset manager as big as BlackRock, this risk is bearable because of all its risk management tools and its hedging investments.

As an asset manager, BlackRock's profit from these investments is ultimately shared between the company itself and the clients who have invested in its funds. Many of these clients are pension funds, and most of the people investing in the funds don't know that they are profiting from a country that can't repay its debt.

As Isaac Mwaipopo, a Zambia Civil Society Debt Alliance member, said: "Zambia's debt crisis is preventing people from getting access to healthcare, education and other social services. We urgently need all of Zambia's lenders, including BlackRock, to agree to cancel debt so we can recover from the Covid pandemic and the economic crisis we face. Loans were given at high interest rates, and have been trading at low prices, so it is only fair lenders agree significant debt cancellation, rather than making mass profit out of the Zambian people."

BlackRock past influence is undeniable, what are the risks for our present economic system?

Part 3:

The political, social, and economic influences of BlackRock. The consequences of a group of entities managing so much wealth.

Part 3: Consequences of BlackRock's influence

BlackRock's current magnitude

The past actions and influences of BlackRock have been discussed, but just how big this firm is haven't yet been understood. What makes it so big and so influential? Why does no one know all of this? What assets does BlackRock own that make the firm so influential and powerful? How does this influence and power transmit to the financial markets and society? Let's delve deeper and see the real consequences of an entity's having concentrated enormous wealth.

According to estimates, there was around 40 trillion in physical money circulating worldwide in 2023 (banknotes and coins, the sum is in dollars), and around 90 trillion if you add bank deposits, traveller's checks, and money market funds[24]. (Assets, stocks, and derivatives are not included, only circulating money). It's tough to have an exact approximation because there is a lot of digital money, cryptocurrencies, fraudulent money, and many

---

[24] Includes investments in Treasury Bills issued by the U.S. Department of the Treasury, commercial paper from corporations, certificates of deposit with fixed maturity dates, repurchase agreements involving the sale and repurchase of securities, short-term government and corporate bonds, and bankers' acceptances.

Part 3: Consequences of BlackRock's influence

transactions are not registered such as OTC[25]. However, looking at these approximative numbers gives us an idea about the size of BlackRock.

BlackRock has around 10 trillion dollars of assets under management. If we do a comparison, BlackRock manages approximately 1/9 of the world's circulating money (BlackRock assets are not all "circulating money", so it doesn't theoretically manage 1/9 of it. It manages 10 trillion of the world's money. However, it gives us an idea of the size of BlackRock.)

Not to mention, Aladdin who manages close to ¼ of the money in circulation worldwide, taking its 2017 AUM when it reached 20 trillion. A former employee said that BlackRock doesn't disclose Aladdin AUM anymore "because of the negative attention the enormous sums attracted." However, A 2020 FT report found that 21.6 trillion dollars came from only ⅓ of Aladdin's 240 clients. Today, that number must be even higher, you just have to take a look at BlackRock's AUM curve.

We can also compare that number to the total equity market capitalisation of the New York Stock Exchange, the largest in the world. According to Statista, it was over 25 trillion dollars in September 2023. Aladdin's total

---

[25] Over the Counter is a term used in finance to describe a transaction, market, or security that is traded between two parties directly and by mutual agreement. This contrasts with transactions made through a centralized and regulated exchange.

Part 3: Consequences of BlackRock's influence

AUM represents as much as the whole capitalisation of NYSE. It is impressive. Every time I read it, I'm shocked.

Consequently, Aladdin controls over half of all ETFs, 17% of the bond market, and 10% of the stock market. Vanguard and State Street Global Advisors, the second-largest fund managers after BlackRock, are all among Aladdin's users, as are half of the top 10 insurers ranked by assets. Japan's $1.5 trillion government pension fund, the largest in the world, also uses the platform. Furthermore, Apple, Microsoft, and Alphabet, the parent company of Google and the three largest publicly traded companies in the United States, all depend on the system to manage and oversee hundreds of billions of dollars within their corporate treasury investment portfolios.

BlackRock owns stocks in approximately 4973 companies, owning a share in the biggest companies such as Apple, Microsoft, Facebook, Amazon, Tesla, Nike, Intel and many more.

A Bloomberg article entitled "The Hidden Dangers of the Great Index Fund Takeover" explains the power of these index fund companies: "As millions of investors have started to invest into index funds, they've also concentrated shareholder power in the Big Three [BlackRock, Vanguard and State Street, (the three biggest investment firms by AUM)]. Some 22% of the shares of the typical S&P 500 company sits in their portfolios, up from 13.5% in 2008. Their power is probably greater, given that many stockholders don't bother to vote their shares. [...] The fund companies combined votes and

Part 3: Consequences of BlackRock's influence

back-channel jawboning, in which they make their views known to directors and chief executive officers, could swing the outcome of important matters such as mergers, major investment decisions, CEO succession, and director elections—even if no fund house has the ability to decide the outcome of such matters alone. They're potentially the most powerful force over a huge swath of America."

The Big Three control more than 80% of the whole ETF industry as of 2021.

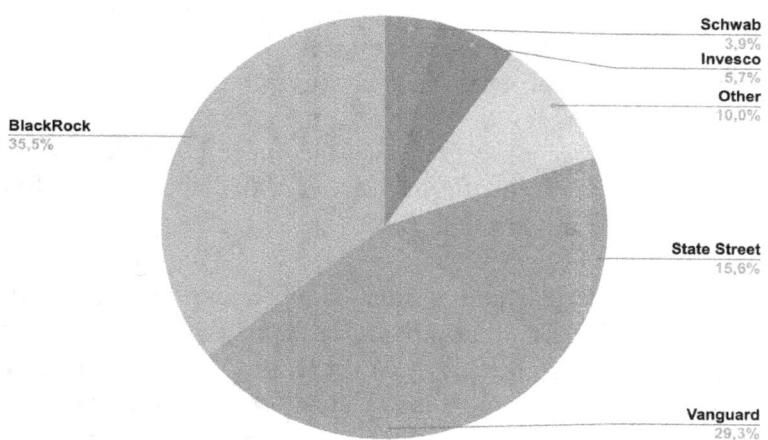

Data: Bloomberg

Being one of the biggest shareholders means having a vote on the decisions of the company's board. The bigger the share, the more influence BlackRock has on the company. The percentage of shares you own corresponds to the

Part 3: Consequences of BlackRock's influence

percentage of votes you have in the company. If you own more than half of the company, you have complete control because your vote counts more than 50%.

Some big companies that BlackRock has ownership of include 6.5% of Apple, 7% of Google, 7% of Microsoft, 7% of Nvidia, 6.5% of JP Morgan, 6.5% of Johnson and Johnson, and many others. A subsequent image will illustrate this very well.

What truly stands out is that BlackRock stands as a shareholder in the foremost companies within every essential, day-to-day use industry:

- In the food industry, it owns a significant share in Coca-Cola and PepsiCo, the two biggest beverage companies.
- In the tech industry, as I mentioned before, it owns a share of Apple, Microsoft, Nvidia, Amazon, Tesla, and Meta.
- In the energy industry, BlackRock invested $170 billion in U.S. public energy companies in 2021 and $85 billion in coal companies.
- In the pharmaceutical industry, BlackRock is a significant shareholder of Johnson and Johnson and other names such as Lonza, the Swiss giant.
- In the digital media industry, BlackRock owns a hefty share in most of the biggest media companies in the US, such as Fox, CBS, CNN, Disney, ... But also in Europe, it owns a share of Bertelsmann, which owns RTL, which holds

Part 3: Consequences of BlackRock's influence

ownership over 45 television stations and 32 radio stations spanning 11 nations. Moreover, Bertelsmann shares co-ownership of the planet's largest book publishing entity, Penguin Random House.
- In the travel industry, BlackRock owns a share in big names such as Boeing, Airbnb, and TripAdvisor.
- In the banking industry, BlackRock owns close to 7% of the seven biggest public banks by assets (JPMorgan, Bank of America, etc)
- In the educational system, BlackRock has investments too. It has created the "BlackRock Impact Opportunities Fund".
- Even in the arms industry, it has a fund with close to a billion invested in nuclear weapons, or holding close to 2.13% of L3Harris Technologies Inc.
- In the cryptocurrency industry, Vanguard owns more than 7% of Coinbase, the largest cryptocurrency exchange, and BlackRock, more than 2%.
- Very recently, Vanguard and BlackRock bought shares in Europe's most valuable firm, Novo Nordisk, which is even more valuable than LVMH. Novo Nordisk is the manufacturer of Wegovy, the new weight loss drug. Vanguard owns more than 3% of it, and BlackRock over 1%.

Part 3: Consequences of BlackRock's influence

They possess a stake in virtually every conceivable sector. They are great at capitalising on future trends - investing in companies or assets that could be prominent.

Last but not least, what is astonishing is that BlackRock is not the only company with so much influence. Vanguard, the second biggest investment firm by AUM, having 7,2 trillion in global assets under management as of December 2022, is one of the biggest shareholders of the companies listed before, and sometimes, it is an even bigger shareholder than BlackRock. BlackRock owns 14.5% of Vanguard, and Vanguard owns 9% of BlackRock. It shows how, in reality, BlackRock possesses even more shares or influence than we would think, through Vanguard. It may not be very big in terms of numbers, but through voting power, it does make a difference. This is the case not only with Vanguard but also with most of the other biggest investment firms.

Omar Chitnis, a Financial Analyst, argues that "they form an immense network comparable to a pyramid. The smaller investors are owned by larger investors. Those are owned by even bigger investors. The visible top of this pyramid shows only two companies whose names we have often seen by now. They are Vanguard and BlackRock".

In essence, BlackRock's magnitude is not just about how much money or assets it manages but its influence over financial markets, corporate behaviour, and even global discussions on policy and sustainability. This colossal

Part 3: Consequences of BlackRock's influence

influence arises mainly from the substantial stakes it holds in the preeminent companies within these diverse industries. Its decisions and strategies have a profound impact on economies and the way businesses operate, making it a powerhouse in the financial world. Even in the absence of mandates from regulatory bodies such as the SEC or other political entities, BlackRock has the influence to enforce actions within companies.

As Charlie Munger, vice-chair of Berkshire Hathaway and Warren Buffett's longtime associate, said to an audience at the Daily Journal Corp. annual meeting: "We have a new bunch of emperors, and they're the people who vote the shares in the index funds. I think the world of Larry Fink, but I'm not sure I want him to be my emperor."

BlackRock's top 25 equity holdings as of Q1 2023
At that time, these 25 positions were worth over $1 trillion and represented about 30% of BlackRock's overall equity portfolio. How much of a controlling stake does BlackRock have in these companies?

Part 3: Consequences of BlackRock's influence

	Exxon Mobil 6.83%	Chevron 7.02%				Energy
		Procter & Gamble Co 6.86%	Coca-Cola Co 7.20%		PepsiCo 7.96%	Consumer staples
	Visa 6.55%	JPMorgan Chase & Co 6.59%	Mastercard 6.89%		Berkshire Hathaway 7.98%	Finance
Tesla 5.70%	Amazon 5.93%			Home Depot 7.60%		Consumer discretionary
Meta 5.69%	Apple 6.54%	Google 7.09%	Broadcom 7.16%	Microsoft 7.22%	Nvidia 7.44%	Technology
Johnson & Johnson 5.46%		Eli Lilly And Co 6.90%		AbbVie 7.86%	UnitedHealth Group 8.02%	Merck & Co 8.24%	Health care

BlackRock biggest equity holding worth **171 billions USD**

Source: Visual Capitalist, "Visualizing BlackRock's Top Equity Holdings"

The next chart from Bloomberg shows the ownership of The Big Three (BlackRock, Vanguard and State Street) across Corporate America. This chart is more representative because the real problem is the influence of these 3 funds together. BlackRock alone is huge, but the combined power of all three is unimaginable.

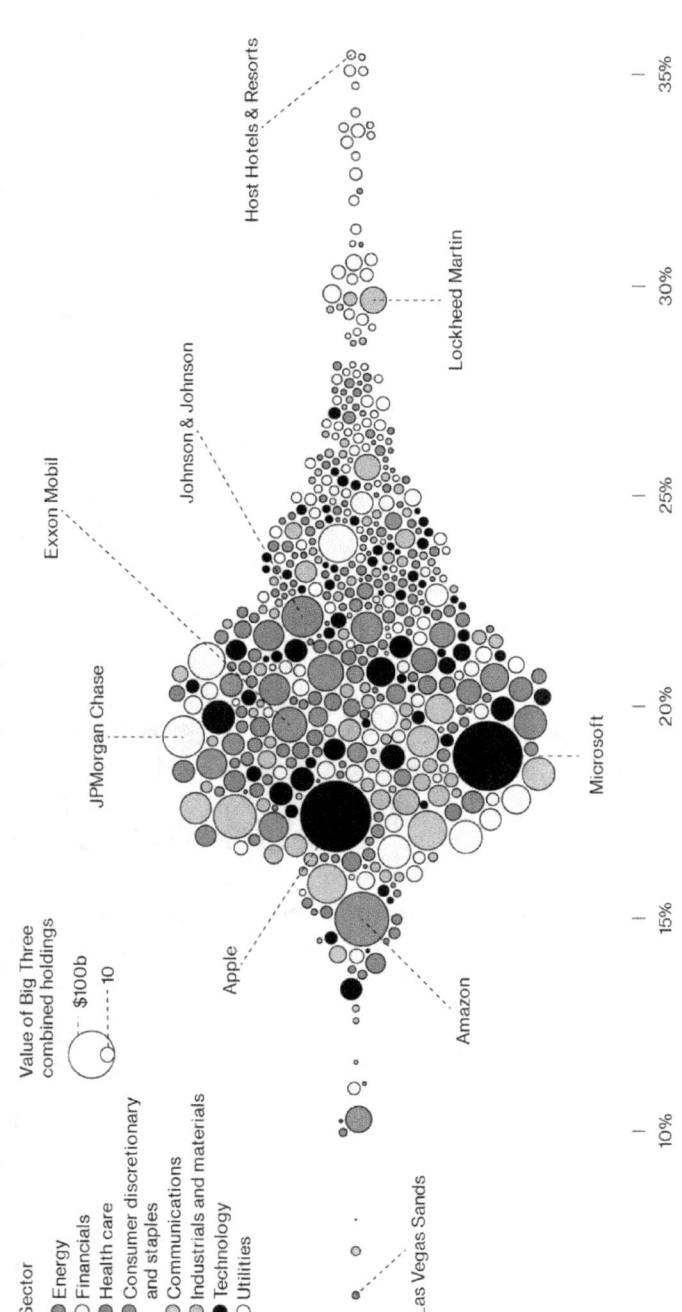

Part 3: Consequences of BlackRock's influence

When researching, I looked at the country where I live, Switzerland. I would never have thought that BlackRock had such extensive ownership in Switzerland. The country is known for its banking secrecy, but where is banking secrecy if the same entity, an American one, owns all the banks?

As stated, BlackRock is very present in Switzerland, holding around 5.8% of all publicly listed companies. Its investments in Swiss companies are among the highest in Europe.

It is the largest disclosed shareholder in Switzerland, meaning it holds the most significant percentage of shares among all the shareholders in a Swiss company or multiple companies. You can see its top Swiss holdings on the subsequent chart.

Swiss companies in which BlackRock has more than 5% ownership as of 2023.

Part 3: Consequences of BlackRock's influence

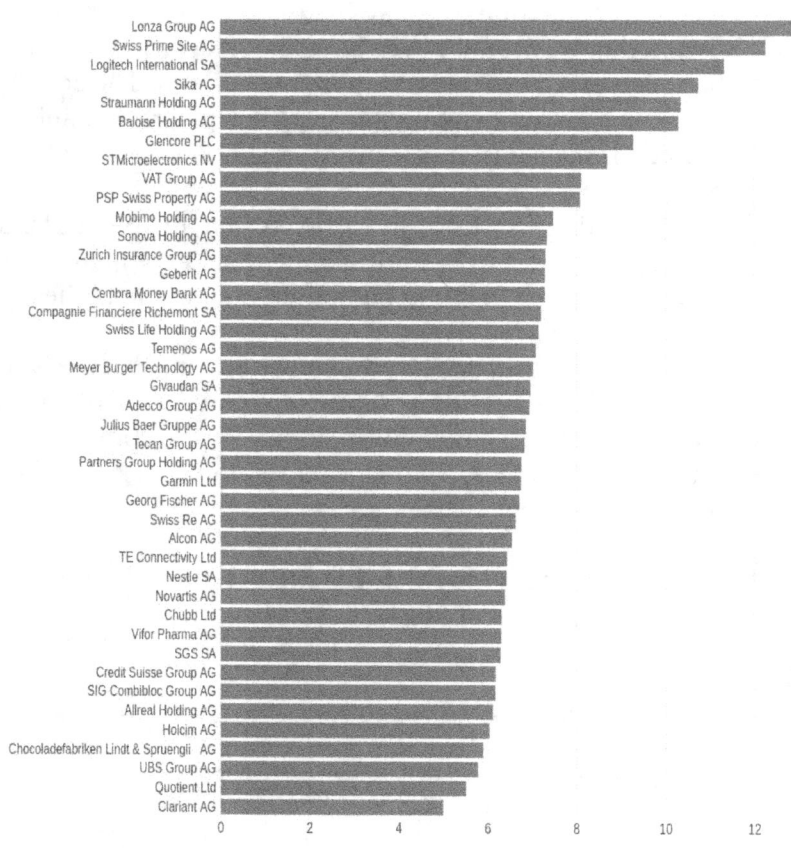

Data: Spotlight on BlackRock

Part 3: Consequences of BlackRock's influence

BlackRock's influence on financial markets, and its ability to influence political institutions.

It is now clear that BlackRock is huge and has shares in every conceivable industry, but to what extent these investments enable it to shape our financial markets and political institutions? The size of BlackRock is a severe problem in this respect. As discussed before, BlackRock is a significant shareholder in most of the biggest companies in the biggest industries. Because of this, BlackRock has a say in the operations of these different companies.

BlackRock's influence on a company and the whole market

A recent example was during COVID-19 when BlackRock tried to change the operations of some companies to benefit others. An interesting quote from an article on Bloomberg from Matt Levine entitled "Money Stuff: You Don't Need Profits Anymore" reflects this situation quite well. Levine often speaks about index funds. His articles are highly pertinent. "Now the whole great big economy is knitted together not only by pricing in product markets but also by common ownership of all the stocks by the same investors, and so you can think of all of the companies—Pfizer, American Airlines, Carnival

Part 3: Consequences of BlackRock's influence

Cruises, The Gap, whoever—as divisions of one giant company, and the one giant company has an executive committee (Larry Fink and the other heads of big investment firms), and the executive committee can tell the divisions (Pfizer, etc.) what to do and how much to charge, and if the giant company's executive committee says "we are going to have our Pfizer division try to find a vaccine and give it away as a loss leader to improve the performance in our other divisions" then, you know, fine, that's how divisions operate, that's how corporate hierarchies go, it's fine. It's not quite like that—there is no giant company, there is no hierarchy—but it is kind of like that, it is enough like that that you ought to start thinking about it, that you ought to think of giant public corporations not as acting on their own pure selfish self-contained profit motives but as part of a vector of interests of their diversified investors, and that you could maybe use that. "Sure, pharmaceutical executive, you say you want to make a big profit on this drug, but what if we asked your owners what they want?"". This quote is terrifying because it shows us how BlackRock can ask or even force a company to do something that may not be productive for the company and may not be what its executives want. However, it will be profitable for BlackRock because most of its investments will perform better if the world is not in a pandemic. BlackRock, owning a share of a company, can shape a decision. Vanguard and State Street are in the same position as BlackRock; they can reach an agreement and vote together. Their vote will count more than that of a

Part 3: Consequences of BlackRock's influence

company's executives because when combined, they sometimes own more than 30% of a company. Then, you must consider that many investors don't actually vote, and others will often follow what index funds do. If BlackRock, Vanguard and State Street vote the same, they will most likely have the majority of the votes. In this way, BlackRock can influence a company's business plan and market.

BlackRock will influence a company's decisions in a manner that may ultimately serve the interests of other companies within its ownership portfolio, as seen in the example above, with Pfizer benefiting most from BlackRock's investments if the vaccine was free. This a threat for our current capitalist economic system.

BlackRock's credibility

BlackRock also influences the financial market just by the decisions it makes. BlackRock is a pioneer in index fund and ETF investing. Its iShares brand is one of the largest ETF providers globally. As these passive investment vehicles track various indices, BlackRock's decisions regarding the composition of these indices can impact the performance of the underlying assets. The sheer size of Blackrock's holdings enables it to impact market prices and liquidity. Blackrock's success is closely tracked by other market participants, meaning that its actions and decisions can have broader implications for the financial system's stability. BlackRock's public statements and commentaries on market trends, economic outlooks, and

Part 3: Consequences of BlackRock's influence

investment strategies influence market sentiment and investor behaviour. When Larry Fink, BlackRock's Chairman, speaks in his annual letters to CEOs, shareholders or investors, everyone listens, analyses carefully and follows what he says. These letters are designed to create instant media coverage. The viewpoints of BlackRock on public policy matters and ideological changes that influence the capital market hold significant sway. As such, politicians and policymakers cannot afford to disregard these perspectives, given their potential impact.

If BlackRock chooses to invest in something new, everyone will follow. If BlackRock doesn't include a company in its fund, people may think it won't perform well, or else BlackRock would have included it. Larry Fink knows he is very influential. He likes to use his influence in public and chooses his words very carefully. He often speaks at events such as the World Economic Forum in Davos. The problem comes when Vanguard, State Street and BlackRock share a common viewpoint and share it to the public. They can by speaking to a few media change the opinion of the whole market.

BlackRock's control over certain domains

On the political side, once again, BlackRock's investments allow it to control certain domains, such as the media. "Vanguard and BlackRock are the top two owners of Time Warner, Comcast, Disney and News Corp, four of the six media companies that control more than 90% of the U.S.

Part 3: Consequences of BlackRock's influence

media landscape." said Jeannette Copperman in a Common Reader article. Aron Vaughan in an article entitled "BlackRock is the Biggest Company You've Never Heard of", affirms that "together, BlackRock and Vanguard own 18% of Fox, 16% of CBS, 13% of Comast — which owns NBC, MSNBC, CNBC, and the Sky media group, 12% of CNN, and 12% of Disney — which owns a number of subsidiaries. Media behemoths that may present themselves as rivals are, in reality, owned by the same company. The editorial authority of BlackRock in the companies in which it has a stake is debatable, but the point is, it can direct narratives globally and influence geopolitics at the grandest of scales".

As a major shareholder in numerous publicly traded companies, BlackRock must vote on important issues during shareholder meetings. While these votes are typically related to corporate governance matters, they can also touch on issues that have broader societal and political implications. BlackRock can use its ownership stake in companies to influence their policies, practices, and governance.

Are index funds empty voters?

Jack Bogle, Vanguard founder and one of the first men to have thought of index funds, warned just before his death in January 2019 that there may be too many shares in too few hands. Index funds are so successful, he wrote in the Wall Street Journal, that they could one day effectively

Part 3: Consequences of BlackRock's influence

control the U.S. stock market. "[He does] not believe that such concentration would serve the national interest."

Most people are not aware that you must choose if you want your share of stocks to be voted by BlackRock. Most are investing through an intermediary such as a commercial bank, an insurance company or a financial advisor and the intermediary buys BlackRock index funds and accepts that BlackRock votes on their behalf because they know that BlackRock will vote in a way to maximise profits. Additionally, voting for your shares is quite time-consuming. No company wants to do that when BlackRock can do it for them. Lastly, voting your shares yourself requires a certain understanding of the companies. Therefore, 95% of BlackRock's institutional index equity assets are eligible for voting choice, and this is not good. It means that all the power and influence that comes from shareholder voting are in the hands of one single entity.

Consequently, the problem of broad diversification arises, meaning mutual funds are often empty voters with an incentive to cast a vote to benefit other investments. In the past, the fact that the biggest shareholder had the biggest interest in the company and would vote accordingly worked. Today, the largest corporate shareholders are widely diversified mutual fund sponsors with interests in the whole fund and not a single company.

Part 3: Consequences of BlackRock's influence

Sean J. Griffith explains this very well in his *"Conflicted Mutual Fund Voting in Corporate Law" paper*. He says: "Most mutual fund sponsors admit that their centralized voting strategy requires them to aggregate all of their funds' votes and cast them uniformly in the way that is most likely to benefit the institution as a whole. In some cases, that would require voting the shares of one company in order to benefit other investments. The clearest examples involve M&A transactions, when mutual funds stand on both sides of the transaction and there can be an obvious winner and loser. Consider a stylized example: Company A management decides to buy Company B, and the merger is viewed by the market as an excellent outcome for Company B, which has been struggling to make interest payments on debt and has had a number of setbacks in the past year. The market is less positive about the prospect for Company A, which will assume many debts and liabilities from Company B. Nonetheless, Company A shareholders overwhelmingly approve the merger. They do not look back even when Company A's share price falls with the announcement of the deal. What is going on here? Company A's ten largest shareholders are sophisticated institutional blockholders—why did they voluntarily agree to a merger that clearly decreased the value of their investment? The answer may be that most of the large institutional investors in Company A also hold large investments in Company B and are therefore hedged. This means that their incentives to oppose the deal may be dampened or even reversed depending on the size of their investment in

Part 3: Consequences of BlackRock's influence

each company. Putting aside the question of whether this is a good outcome for the institution's investors, it is unlikely to be in the best interest of the Company A shareholders, who now hold less valuable stock."

There are some prominent examples, such as Tesla's acquisition of SolarCity, and Bank of America's plan to acquire FleetBoston, etc.

In a 2018 paper, professors Ryan Bubb and Emiliano Catan found that the Big Three were unlikely to oppose management on hot-button issues such as executive pay and likely to support management proposals to merge or make large acquisitions. BlackRock supported such merger and acquisition proposals 79% of the time. The inability of the management teams of a company to get a merger transaction done, unless the biggest shareholders (BlackRock, Vanguard and State Street) agree, is one of the many ways in which they can exert their influence. The power of a public listed company does not lie in the hands of the executives anymore but in the hands of the biggest shareholders (the index funds).

Index funds find themselves in a complex situation. On one hand, they represent a concentration of wealth in a select few entities, thereby wielding considerable influence and power. However, on the other side, passivity and inadequate governance activity issues arise. If these funds do not exert their governance influence, it leads to a state of passivity, which is equally undesirable. This

Part 3: Consequences of BlackRock's influence

delicate balance presents a challenging scenario for index funds. In both cases, they are often criticised.

BlackRock's way of working as a shareholder is stated in their "Investment Stewardship" and "Engagement Priorities". As of March 2023, it says, "As one of many, and typically a minority shareholder, BIS [BlackRock Investment Stewardship] does not tell companies what to do. Our role, on behalf of our clients as long-term shareholders, is to better understand how company leadership is managing risks and capitalizing on opportunities to help protect and enhance the financial interests of their investors." "We engage, as necessary, with members of the board's nominating and/or governance committee to assess whether governance practices and board composition are appropriate given the business and the broader context in which the company operates."

However, "Index fund managers may follow passive investment strategies, but they don't blindly choose stocks and sit back", says John Coates. "Fund companies have multiple tools to influence corporate behavior, such as developing preferred policies on executive compensation, carbon footprints, gender diversity, and other governance matters. They often do this in coordination with other industry leaders", Coates says. "A small number of unelected agents, operating largely behind closed doors, are increasingly important to the lives of millions who barely know of the existence much less the identity or inclinations of those agents."

Part 3: Consequences of BlackRock's influence

This quote from John Coates as written in the article: "The Hidden Dangers of the Great Index Fund Takeover" by Bloomberg reflects the fact that we have no idea what happens behind those "doors". We know these agents are influential. However, we have no idea of their intentions. He also speaks about Fund companies developing "preferred policies". What are those?

Why is ESG so popular?

BlackRock has become more active as a shareholder lately, pushing for ESG (Environmental, Social, and Governance). ESG is one of those "preferred policies" that John Coates speaks about. ESG is a score that highlights how much a company is doing environmentally, socially, and governmentally. The higher the score is, the more investors are attracted to a company. Lately, it has become a significant factor to consider for companies. As Larry Fink said, according to Reuters at a speaking event in Davos, "If you do not have a lens towards decarbonisation, you're not going to win one euro of business." Pushing for ESG, BlackRock is pouring huge sums into political and advertising campaigns. We are getting advertisements on climate change, and BlackRock is doing it to make money. Is ESG just another business policy to find a new way to collect money from clients? It is known that ESG is becoming increasingly popular among investors. It, therefore, presents a big business opportunity for

Part 3: Consequences of BlackRock's influence

BlackRock to collect new fees from their existing clients and get new clients via their advertisements. Some are already pulling their money from BlackRock such as the Republican state pension funds that announced in March 2024 the withdrawal of $13.3bn.

Let's look at some numbers. According to BlackRock's "2023 Investment Stewardship Voting Spotlight", BlackRock engaged in 4000 different matters for 2642 different companies, covering 49 markets, from July 1, 2022, through June 30, 2023. BlackRock has a very significant governing role in our economy. Larry Fink ironically said in his 2023 Annual Chairman Letter to Investors: "It is for governments to make policy and enact legislation, and not for companies, including asset managers, to be the environmental police."

Engagements across BlackRock's five priorities

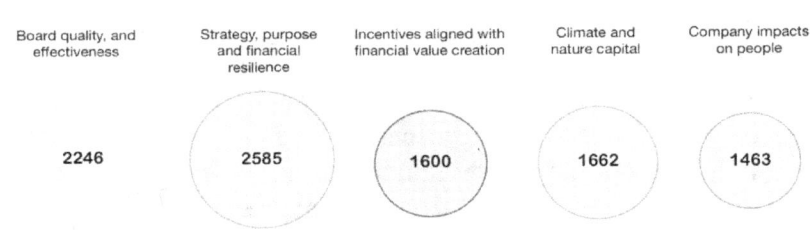

Board quality, and effectiveness	Strategy, purpose and financial resilience	Incentives aligned with financial value creation	Climate and nature capital	Company impacts on people
2246	2585	1600	1662	1463

Data: BlackRock's 2023 Investment Stewardship Voting Spotlight

(Many discussions about engagement touch upon various subjects, which means that the cumulative sum of

Part 3: Consequences of BlackRock's influence

engagements related to the top five priority areas may not equal the total engagements conducted.)

If we look at the support of BlackRock, it varies greatly between management proposals and shareholder proposals. BlackRock didn't support management recommendations only 12% of the time. However, BlackRock's voting decisions on shareholder proposals in the following domains: governance, company impact on people, climate and natural capital were against 742 times and for only 71 times. The mentioned domains are hot ESG topics.

This difference may be attributed to the following reasons. Proposals from a company's management are usually the result of comprehensive strategic planning by the board and executives, who possess in-depth knowledge of the company's operations. These proposals often reflect the company's long-term goals and strategies.

In contrast, shareholder proposals originate from a wide array of shareholders. These shareholders may have varying levels of understanding and control over the company's operations. Furthermore, their primary focus might be on their individual profits rather than ESG issues, which could influence the nature and quality of their proposals.

This difference in focus and understanding can lead to a significant divergence between management and shareholder proposals.

Part 3: Consequences of BlackRock's influence

These numbers show that BlackRock actively manages some companies in which it has a share. Even if some of these main priorities are positive in nature, the fact that BlackRock owns so many other companies creates a conflict of interest, as previously seen. BlackRock's vote is always cast to benefit its other assets, and most importantly, to make a profit.

By pushing for ESG, BlackRock seeks to enhance the appeal of the companies it invests in, setting a standard that other investors and the public increasingly recognise as important. This influence helps BlackRock distinguish itself from competitors and potentially increase its profits. As Larry Fink said in his Annual Chairman Letter to Investors: "Some of the most attractive investment opportunities in the years ahead will be in the transition finance space. Given its importance to our clients, BlackRock's ambition is to be the leading investor in these opportunities on their behalf.". Firms don't follow narratives for the good cause, they are not angels, if there are opportunities in the transition space, they will follow this narrative. BlackRock was the one that started this investment narrative and leads it now. If you don't do what BlackRock does, then you lose. Aligning your actions with the industry's most influential entities is a key to success, that's what investors tells you to do.

Larry Fink, wrote two letters in 2020, saying in the first that "In the near future – and sooner than most anticipate – there will be a significant reallocation of capital", and in the second letter, BlackRock pushed for sustainable

Part 3: Consequences of BlackRock's influence

investing: "We believe that sustainability should be our new standard for investing". BlackRock's promotion of ESG investing has been driven, in part, by the inclusion of ESGU (BlackRock ESG fund) in model portfolios, effectively making it a self-fulfilling prophecy. Many investors may have entered ESGU without actively choosing it as an investment strategy, raising questions about the true impact of ESG investments and their fees on investors and society. It raises concerns about whether BlackRock's promotion of ESG is solely aimed at gaining new fees from investors.

Every company gets an ESG rating so investors can judge its ESG impact. However, a Bloomberg investigation found that the ESG ratings used to justify ESGU's sustainability label mainly assess the potential harm to companies' bottom lines due to government regulations and other factors, primarily related to climate change, rather than their actual environmental and social impact. These ratings come from MSCI Inc., BlackRock's largest customer, and have allowed the BlackRock ESG fund to hold companies that some consider as environmental and social offenders, including fossil fuel giants like Chevron and Exxon Mobil, along with Facebook (Meta Platforms), Amazon, McDonald's, and JP Morgan Chase. This investigation raises further questions about the true intentions of BlackRock's ESG commitment.

In January 2024, BlackRock Investment Stewardship resumes its engagement priorities for the year as follows:

Part 3: Consequences of BlackRock's influence

"1. Board quality and effectiveness
2. Strategy, purpose, and financial resilience
3. Incentives aligned with financial value creation
4. Climate and natural capital
5. Company impacts on people"

There is little difference compared to other years. BlackRock remains big on ESG.

In conclusion, the rise of ESG priorities and BlackRock's active engagement further demonstrate its ability to shape corporate behaviour, public perception, or investor sentiment. Questions about the true intentions behind BlackRock ESG initiatives and the impact of its actions on society and investors, as well as the impact it will have on political institutions, given its substantial financial influence, raise concerns about transparency and accountability within the financial industry.

The Engine, Exxon example: how a few firms and ESG can change a board of directors

There has been much discussion, yet examples are scarce. Here, however, is a notable instance where not just BlackRock, but a consortium of the most prominent investment firms collectively swayed the outcome of a shareholder's vote.

A small investing firm unknown by most before this event, Engine No.1, wanted to install three new directors

Part 3: Consequences of BlackRock's influence

on the board of Exxon, the energy giant, to reduce the carbon footprint of Exxon. Nobody believed the small firm stood a chance until the three biggest investing firms (BlackRock, Vanguard, and State Street) gave their vote in support of Engine No.1. We can't know exactly why the big three gave their support. However, just like that, a tiny investing firm completely changed the board of one of the biggest companies in the energy industry. According to a New York Times article entitled, "Exxon Mobil Defeated by Activist Investor Engine No. 1", "Engine No. 1 held only 0.02 percent of Exxon's shares, giving it a similar portion of proxy votes, while those three institutional investors together accounted for nearly 20 percent of the voting shares."

This example highlights a potential threat to democracy in the context of corporate governance and shareholder activism. It goes against many ideas about democracy.

The ability of investors to guide corporate decisions can potentially be exploited for personal or narrow group interests. The risk is that well-funded firms might exert undue influence over a company's direction, not necessarily for the greater good of the company, its employees, or the wider economy.

This situation prompts discussions about the appropriate balance of power and accountability within corporations and how to ensure that shareholder activism genuinely benefits the larger goals of the company, its shareholders, and society.

Mr. Park, a former BlackRock employee, said: "The days are over where you could think, you know, these

Part 3: Consequences of BlackRock's influence

guys would give the benefit of the doubt to management." Times have changed. In the past, investors would let the company run itself. Now, investors are taking active management positions in companies, casting their votes in their self-interest.

The issue is that the ratios of the shares these well-funded investors own are getting bigger. More and more people are investing in index funds, and investing algorithms like Aladdin are not accessible to the public, so private investors must go through them, too. The problem is that one day, the Big Three's shares will exceed 50% in some prominent companies and industries. That day, the three biggest funds will have total control over companies if they vote the same way. This presents a serious concern for the future of our economy.

In 2020, the Big Three combined were already the largest shareholder in 96% of Fortune 250 companies, and almost 90% of S&P 500 firms. This concentration of corporate ownership has significant implications for corporate governance and competition.

BlackRock's influence on political elections

Furthermore, BlackRock also influences political elections. BlackRock's political action committee has been actively contributing to political campaigns. From January 2021 to the middle of October, it donated approximately $647,000 to various congressional candidates, their leadership PACs (PACs organised by politicians), and political parties. BlackRock executives

Part 3: Consequences of BlackRock's influence

make contributions to the company's PAC, which then determines which campaigns to support, and they also have the option to contribute to campaigns personally. It is important because BlackRock's own PAC can donate to candidates or parties with the same ideologies as them, which will support them. However, it is important to note that these funds do not come from the BlackRock corporate fund but from its PAC. Its PAC raises money from shareholders, members, or employees. Also, a PAC is much more regulated.

BlackRock's little-known influence on central banks

Finally, one influence that must be discussed is that of BlackRock on some central banks. For example, let's take the Federal Reserve System. The Federal Reserve System is structured around 12 Reserve Banks, each in a different city across the United States. Commercial banks within the jurisdiction of each Reserve Bank and that are part of the Federal Reserve System play a role in its governance. These commercial banks are responsible for electing six of the nine directors that make up the board of each Reserve Bank. BlackRock, being a shareholder of most of these commercial banks, can indirectly influence the board of directors of the Reserve Banks of The Federal Reserve System.

Part 3: Consequences of BlackRock's influence

How is each Reserve Bank board of directors elected?

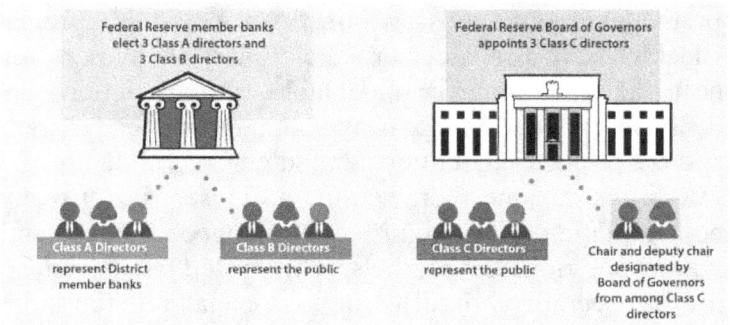

Source: Roles and Responsibilities of Federal Reserve Directors

There are also central banks that are wholly owned by private sector entities, such as the Banca d'Italia. In Switzerland, The Swiss National Bank (SNB) is owned by a mix of public and private entities. Around 78% of it is owned by Swiss public entities; the rest are publicly traded on SIX (the Swiss stock exchange). BlackRock is the largest shareholder in Switzerland. Indirectly, it has a little influence on one of the most important institutions in Switzerland. Its influence may not be as significant as in other fields; however, it demonstrates how BlackRock is everywhere.

Part 3: Consequences of BlackRock's influence

To conclude

In the evolving landscape of finance and investment, BlackRock's influence on the financial market and political institutions is undeniable, and its actions and decisions will continue to shape both the financial markets and the political institutions that intersect with them.

As this chapter draws to a close, it provokes contemplation on the significant influence of index funds within our financial markets. Their relentless pursuit of profits, seemingly indifferent to societal repercussions, raises critical questions. Could this unyielding drive inadvertently exacerbate social and economic disparities, thereby widening the wealth gap? This concern is particularly poignant for low-income communities, who may find themselves further marginalized in this financial landscape.

Part 3: Consequences of BlackRock's influence

BlackRock's influence on social and economic inequality

Could BlackRock influence social and economic development so that its decisions could give an advantage to some people and a disadvantage to others?

As John Coates says in a Harvard interview: "Index funds have a complicated effect on inequality. On the one hand, they allow ordinary working-class Americans to more cost effectively diversify their investments for retirement and put it into the stock market in a way that would be maybe too expensive for them to do if they tried to do it in some other way. And since owning stocks, at least in our country, has typically produced higher returns than other kinds of saving, that is a source of reducing inequality, because it allows more people to get the benefit of rising capital prices. So, if you're out of the stock market, you're going to get left behind in the U.S. economy. On the other hand, not everyone has enough money even to use index funds. I mean, there are millions of Americans who have no investments at all. And so, in that way, index funds further intensify the spread between those who are left out entirely of the private investment part of our economy and those who are in it."

Part 3: Consequences of BlackRock's influence

Total net asset under management of Exchange Traded Funds in the United States from 2002 to 2022.

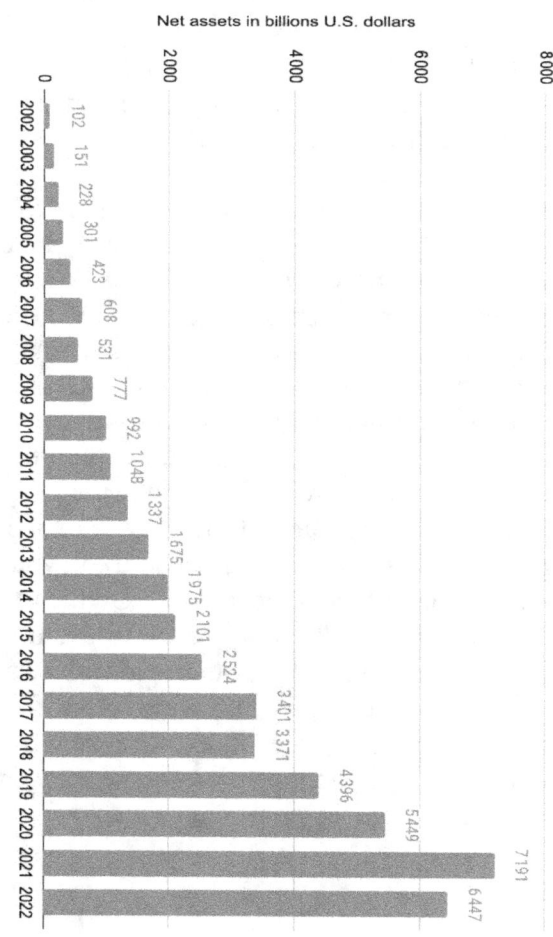

Data: Statista Research

Part 3: Consequences of BlackRock's influence

Different interests

Consequently, Leo Strine Jr., a respected figure in corporate law and the former chief justice of the Delaware Supreme Court, spoke about the conflict that could come from people investing their retirement in these funds. He wrote an interesting paper entitled: "Fiduciary Blind Spot: The Failure of Institutional Investors to Prevent the Illegitimate Use of Working Americans' Savings for Corporate Political Spending".

First, he discusses how we became "forced capitalists" because of the decline of defined benefits pension plans and the rise of 401(k)s[26]. Everyone started investing in these funds. As an ordinary person, you have no choice or even strong incentives to give funds every month to institutional investors. Strine argues that we became "forced capitalists" despite relying on our capacity to sell our labour and secure quality employment for economic stability. We primarily invest for two objectives: funding our children's higher education and ensuring our financial well-being during retirement. The problem is that the money is trapped until retirement age because of tax

---

[26] A 401(k) is a tax-advantaged retirement savings plan offered by employers in the United States, allowing employees to contribute a portion of their pre-tax income to individual investment accounts, often with employer matching contributions, for the purpose of building savings for retirement.

Part 3: Consequences of BlackRock's influence

policies. You have no control over the investments made with it. (You don't pay income taxes on the money if you wait until retirement before withdrawing the money).

His argument is based on the idea that while individual companies may benefit from engaging in political spending to influence lawmakers and government policies, index funds, as asset managers, should consider the broader interests of their fund shareholders. Many of these shareholders are regular workers who invest in 401(k) retirement plans, trusting that the index funds will act in their best interests. He points out that when companies use their financial resources to support lawmakers who advocate for policies that grant businesses more power over matters such as employee compensation and benefits, it can ultimately result in adverse consequences for workers.

Index funds like BlackRock and Vanguard should be more proactive in overseeing the political activities of the companies they invest in to ensure that these activities align with the long-term financial interests of the fund's shareholders, many of whom are everyday workers saving for their retirement.

To sum up, there are so many different types of people investing in these index funds, meaning that in the same fund, there is the money of a person saving for retirement, the money of a wealthy person or even the money of an institutional investor, and therein lies the problem. First, all of these people have different interests. Yes, they do all invest, hopefully, to make a profit. However, the person saving for retirement wouldn't want the minimum

Part 3: Consequences of BlackRock's influence

wage lowered, even if his retirement savings could be just a little more because the companies in the fund might perform a bit better. On the other hand, the institutional investors would want that. What will BlackRock do in this situation? It will rarely look at the interests of the people investing in the fund, it can't, it will look at how it can be more profitable. If the companies in the fund must pay lower wages, they will have higher profits, leading to the fund making more money. If the funds make more money annually, they can charge higher fees. Therefore, BlackRock, having the right to vote on behalf of its clients, will vote to make the company more profitable. The problem is that it will mostly affect the people who are highly dependent on the economic circumstances, which depend on minimum wages, labour conditions, inflation, etc. These people are often disadvantaged communities or low-income individuals. Therefore, it creates a new inequality and widens the income gap.

Anat Admati, a Stanford finance and economics professor, says fund companies should use their leverage to ensure corporations are managed in the true interests of a fund's clients: "Start with the basics, such as ensuring better controls to prevent fraud, deception, reckless practices, and political activities against the public interest [...] and it's just possible that competition will improve and costly scandals, such as the opioid epidemic, Boeing Co.'s 737 Max failure, Wells Fargo & Co.'s fraudulent checking accounts, and Facebook Inc.'s repeated privacy breaches may not happen or decrease."

Part 3: Consequences of BlackRock's influence

Aladdin's Monopoly

Furthermore, Aladdin, BlackRock's investment algorithm, creates some sort of inequality too, a more institutional inequality that indirectly affects investors. Aron Vaughan, a journalist, explains it well: "If Aladdin's network were to be hacked, it could have a swift and catastrophic impact on the global economy. The more existential problem is the monopoly this algorithm has created. BlackRock essentially rents out its proprietary golden goose to the world's highest bidders — mostly large hedge funds and megabanks. This paradigm leaves smaller investors at a major disadvantage and gives companies like BlackRock and Vanguard licence to steer the economy as they see fit. The success Aladdin had in almost single-handedly stopping the world from experiencing complete financial collapse [during the financial crisis of 2008] earned it a prestigious place among the world's governing bodies. Aladdin was given free rein to decide what to do with the $2 trillion that was printed in the wake of the Great Recession [the 2008 crisis]. The majority of it was allocated to bonds and funding to prop up the mortgage companies and banks — assets in which BlackRock was already heavily invested."

Aladdin has created an institutional inequality. The biggest funds, companies, and governments will bid high enough to enjoy its benefits, and everybody else is left behind. Aladdin manages the money of the biggest banks in the world. Most of the time, it allocates the funds it must

Part 3: Consequences of BlackRock's influence

benefit the people using it. As said, it has created a monopoly, and those who can't bid high enough to use it are kept out of the market.

We have seen that, even governments have asked for Aladdin's help during several crises. On those occasions, Aladdin's investments benefited a small part of the population, creating an advantage for some - the ones having money invested in BlackRock - and a disadvantage to others, the ones unable to use that technology since they were neither clients of BlackRock nor clients of institutions using Aladdin. The worst was for those not even able to invest any money in the stock market. All of this resulted in some people being left behind after the crises.

Inequality on asset price inflation

Investment fund companies can also influence social and economic inequality indirectly through asset inflation. When central banks "print money", they typically do so by engaging in quantitative easing (QE). The goal of QE is to inject money into the economy to stimulate economic activity and prevent deflation during times of economic downturn. By purchasing government bonds and other assets, central banks increase the demand for these assets, which drives their prices and lowers their yields (interest rates). Lower interest rates make borrowing cheaper for individuals and businesses, encouraging spending, investment, and borrowing.

Part 3: Consequences of BlackRock's influence

People who can borrow in these times (often bad) where interest rates are very low or even negative and then invest that money, will have a considerable benefit in confronting others suffering from the economic downturn and cannot borrow money or even invest what they have. This is because when bond prices rise, their yields (interest rates) fall. This prompts investors to seek higher returns on other assets, such as stocks and corporate bonds. It can increase the prices of these assets, benefiting investors such as BlackRock, who own these assets. In 2020, during the Covid pandemic, when the Fed made its purchases of corporate bonds ETFs, almost half of the Fed's purchases went into BlackRock funds, according to ETFGI, an ETF research and consulting firm.

What is important to note as well is that BlackRock influences some central banks or what is more probable, advise them, as discussed previously. Therefore, it can influence a central bank's decision-making to derive the most benefit for itself.

To conclude

Most of the economic and social influences of BlackRock come from the consequences of asset prices rising or falling. The wealth effect from rising asset prices benefits those already owning substantial assets, potentially exacerbating income inequality. Then, the low interest rates and increased liquidity resulting from central bank actions can encourage excessive risk-taking and asset price bubbles. Not always, but often, the people suffering

Part 3: Consequences of BlackRock's influence

most from such bubbles are the investors who are too late and generally don't invest. Still, some may have heard in the news or from their friends and colleagues that there was a lifetime opportunity, so they invested their savings. Big investors such as BlackRock usually follow what their algorithm says and have hedging investments. When the bubble burst, the people who were too late lost all their savings. They were the most negatively affected ones.

In brief, BlackRock does not have much of a direct influence on social and economic inequality. Its influence mostly comes from the consequences of its shareholder votes, investments, or the monopoly Aladdin created.

The worst inequality it has created is when people have to use one of these largest funds for their investments, as not to do so would put them at a disadvantage compared to those who do use them. Given this current trajectory and the increasing demand for its services, we can anticipate that BlackRock will continue to expand over time. This growth is expected in terms of the company's size and assets under management, as well as its client base. Therefore, the problem of wealth concentration, power, and influence can only worsen.

Part 4:

The future of our economic system. Are there any solutions?

Part 4: The future

What role could BlackRock play in the future?

In an age dominated by capitalism, the role of BlackRock, a colossal institutional investor, is a pivotal question for the future. Traditional capitalism thrives on competitive companies striving for profits as they tackle societal challenges. However, an alternative approach suggests that common ownership by institutional investors could offer a new way to capture value.

BlackRock's substantial ownership stakes in major corporations, such as tech giants like Apple, Microsoft, Nvidia, and Google, illustrate this common ownership trend. While index funds like the S&P 500 simplify investment and reduce risk, they encourage collective success over individual competition.

This raises a critical question: does widespread common ownership slow innovation and economic competitiveness? The increasing popularity of index funds over individual stocks amplifies this concern. Large ETFs benefit from economies of scale, offering lower costs and increased liquidity, which can reinforce the dominance of a select few, including BlackRock.

As institutional ownership grows and more investors embrace index funds for their cost-efficiency and liquidity benefits, the future appears poised for a smaller number of major players, such as BlackRock, to wield greater economic influence.

Part 4: The future

Future growth

BlackRock, most of the time, owns a big share of the major corporations in the same industry. Take the tech industry, for example; BlackRock owns a big share of Apple, Microsoft, Nvidia, and Google. According to research led by Harvard law professor Einer Elhauge, this common ownership in many industries constitutes a huge threat to the competitiveness of today's economy. Index funds are great for investors because of their simplicity and diversity, but this diversification is great for investors mostly because of the anti-competitive effects.

If a private investor buy shares of Apple, he would like it to take risks, invest in new technologies, and crush its competitors. However, if an investor invests in the S&P 500, it means he has simultaneous investments in Apple, Microsoft and other big tech companies. This investor would never want Apple to crush its competitors. He would rather have all the tech companies in the S&P 500 flourish together without any fighting between companies. This shows how anti-productive common ownership is on a big scale. In addition, more investors have been investing in index funds since August 2019 rather than individual stocks. As of August 31, 2019, index funds held $4.27 trillion in assets, compared to $4.25 trillion in active funds. This gap is getting bigger, and it will highly affect our economy.

An ETF with assets of $10 billion would have one hundred times the assets under management of an ETF with assets of $100 million tracking the same index. However, the costs of operating the former would likely be much less than one hundred times the cost of operating the latter. These economies of scale provide the operator of the $10 billion ETF with a structural advantage over the operator of the $100 million ETF: the former can charge investors a much smaller expense ratio to cover costs and also offer beneficial investors significant liquidity advantages. Investors considering ETF investments will consider not only the fees charged by the investment manager but also the bid-ask spreads that the investor will face when they acquire and dispose of their investment in the ETF.

Large institutional investors are increasing their ownership of company shares, which is likely to continue. Small institutional investors do not have many chances to flourish, as just seen. Large institutional investors are investing more in index funds, which have become popular due to their low costs and ease of use. So, it suggests that the top three investors will only become more influential in time, which is scary. The following graph shows this well.

Nonetheless, it is important to consider that a significant number of investors and shareholders often abstain from voting their shares. This abstention effectively amplifies the influence of those shareholders who participate in voting. Consequently, the voting power of active shareholders is disproportionately higher. The 30%

ownership becomes a 40% one. Their ownership is more significant than any official numbers.

Expected future growth of the Big Three (BlackRock, Vanguard, State Street) combined voting stake of S&P 500 companies.

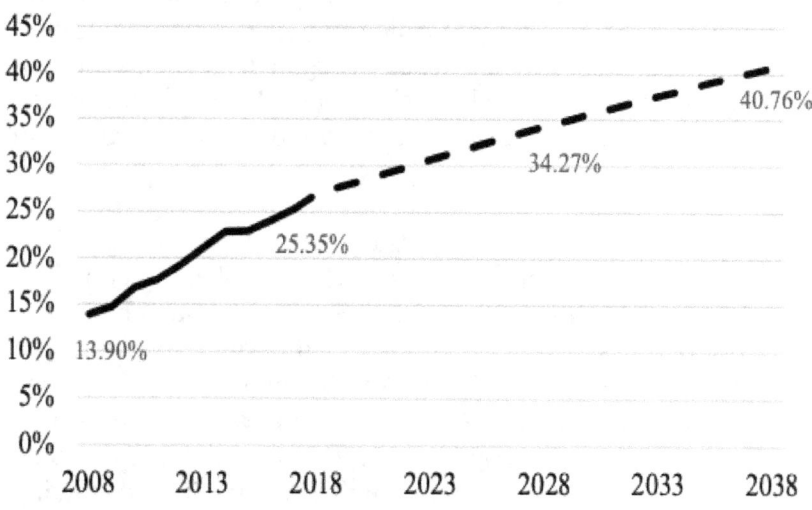

Graph from a 2019 article of the Boston University Law Review, "The Specter of The Giant Three" by Lucian Bebchuk.

Part 4: The future

The estimated average share of S&P 500 companies that the Big Three own, measured as a percentage of the total votes cast at annual meetings from 2007 to 2021.

	BlackRock	Vanguard	SSGA	Total
2007	5.2%	3.5%	3.8%	12.5%
2008	6.1%	3.9%	4.5%	14.5%
2009	7.5%	5.0%	4.9%	17.4%
2010	7.3%	5.5%	5.0%	17.8%
2011	7.2%	6.0%	5.0%	18.2%
2012	7.3%	6.6%	5.5%	19.4%
2013	7.5%	7.5%	5.7%	20.7%
2014	7.6%	8.1%	5.7%	21.4%
2015	8.0%	8.9%	5.4%	22.3%
2016	8.3%	10.0%	5.8%	24.1%
2017	8.8%	10.9%	5.7%	25.4%
2018	9.2%	11.8%	5.5%	26.5%
2019	9.6%	12.4%	5.7%	27.7%
2020	9.5%	11.8%	5.5%	26.8%
2021	9.8%	12.0%	5.7%	27.5%

Table from a 2022 Harvard paper, "Big Three Power, and Why it Matters" by Lucian Bebchuk and Scott Hirst.

Part 4: The future

The emerging problems

After having observed the possible future growth of index funds, two questions arise:
- First, what will the Big Three do when their combined voting shares are higher than 50%, meaning they have complete control over some of the biggest companies in the world?
- Second, how will our capitalist economy and democratic society evolve with this threat?

Matt Levine has a very pertinent view about common ownership. In a Bloomberg article he explains: "Solving any big societal problem is generally a high-stakes competitive endeavor for the for-profit companies looking to do it, and that this might not always be good for the world. But it is the normal way we structure capitalist society, and usually we think that it's pretty good. There's a thing that people want, and if you build it you will add a lot of value to the world; you will be able to sell the thing at a price that reflects that value, and capture some of that value for yourself in the form of profits. This is good for you because you get rich, but it's good for society because it provides incentives: You will work hard to invent things that people want, because the more they want them, the more money you can make. This is basic capitalism stuff. The argument that I am making here, though, is that common ownership by institutional investors provides another way for companies to capture the value of what

Part 4: The future

they do, besides selling it for a profit. If you build a thing that people want, if you make customers better off, if you add value to the world, you can internalize that value not by charging people for it but by owning all your customers, or rather by having the same owners as your customers. Someone else benefits from the thing you make; they capture all of the surplus, and you capture none of it, but it's fine, because you and they are in some sense the same person. You all work for the same super-company—the company of the index funds—and so you are motivated to pursue the common good rather than your own individual profit. Maybe the index funds really are the vanguard of socialism."

In a Jacobin interview with leftist economist J.W. Mason about "finance's role in capitalist society", Mason points out: "If all the companies are owned by the same handful of big diversified investing institutions, and if those institutions have no interest in competition between the companies they own, then what is the point of capitalism?"

Matt Levine, again in a Bloomberg article titled: "Are index funds communist?", points out an interesting fact about the future of our economic and social system: "Index funds are in many ways a perfection of financial capitalism: Not only are they the result of scientific finance (modern portfolio theory, the efficient markets hypothesis, etc.) replacing earlier and less rigorous forms of investing, but they also concentrate and align

Part 4: The future

shareholders with each other, and corporate managers with shareholders, in a way that seems like it would be well suited to "ensure that corporations remain within capitalist logic." And the result is something that both Marxists and also financial analysts think is quasi-communist, that "undermines the basic logic that made capitalism an economically and politically successful system in the first place." What if Marx was right that capitalism would ultimately destroy itself, but the way that it does so is through index funds?"

Levine's idea, in essence, is that index funds align the interests of shareholders (investors) with each other and with corporate managers by passively tracking market indices. This alignment may create a quasi-communist dynamic where wealth and power become concentrated in a way that undermines the competitive nature of capitalism. The rise of index funds is seen as potentially undermining the fundamental logic that has made capitalism economically and politically successful. Concentrating ownership and encouraging passive investing might contribute to wealth concentration and reduce the innovation traditionally associated with capitalism.

Levine's argument suggests a paradox where index funds, a product of capitalism, might inadvertently hasten capitalism's self-destructive tendencies, as predicted by Karl Marx. Marx believed capitalism would eventually lead to its own downfall due to inherent contradictions and inequalities within the system. Marx was one of the main actors in the economic debate at the end of the 19th century. It was believed that either a tiny group of individuals would control most firms or the wealth underlying these firms would become increasingly concentrated in the hands of fewer people. The latter is starting to be seen with the biggest investment firms. It is important to note that it would erode the fundamental principles that have historically made capitalism prosperous and politically viable in either scenario.

Index funds, by seeking the common good of each company, contradict a fundamental concept of capitalism as articulated by Adam Smith in his seminal work, *An Inquiry into the Nature and Causes of the Wealth of Nations*. Smith posits that an individual, by pursuing their own interest, often promotes societal welfare more effectively than when they consciously aim to do so. He expresses scepticism towards those who claim to trade for the public good. "By pursuing his own interest (the individual) frequently promotes that of the society more effectually than when he really intends to promote it. I have never known much good done by those who affected to trade for the public good."

However, it's important to note that the operation of index funds could also be viewed as a manifestation of the self-interest principle. Fund managers aim to maximise returns for their investors (and, by extension, for themselves), and investors choose index funds to secure reliable returns. But this is theory. In practice, by trying to maximise the profits of all their investors, index funds must pursue the common good of each company in the fund to be able to satisfy all their clients. Investors may

Part 4: The future

pursue their own interests, but the fund can't. It must pursue the good of all those investing in the fund and all the companies appertaining to it. It doesn't seem capitalist at all.

As Larry Fink, in his 2022 Letter to CEOs, confirms: "In today's globally interconnected world, a company must create value for and be valued by its full range of stakeholders[27] in order to deliver long-term value for its shareholders. Putting your company's purpose at the foundation of your relationships with your stakeholders is critical to long-term success." You must therefore pursue all stakeholders' common good if you want to achieve long-term success. What are all the index funds stakeholders common good? Pure profits. They all invest their money in the fund hoping higher returns. The index funds must deliver. Is this long term possible?

Capitalism, as we used to know it, has undergone a transformation. Can we turn back the clock or at least make it work? Is it possible? Are there solutions to the problem raised by this transformation, or should we look

---

[27] Stakeholders are individuals, groups, or entities with an interest or concern in the activities, outcomes, or success of a business or project. They can include employees, customers, investors, suppliers, the community, and other parties who may be affected by or can affect the organisation's decisions and performance.

to embrace it? Perhaps this new system holds unseen potential. Let's look at it from a new perspective.

Part 4: The future

Possible solutions

To sum up, the problem is the following: there is one entity, in this example: BlackRock, controlling too much wealth. Investments in so many different fields and companies allow BlackRock to influence the financial markets, political institutions and our daily lives. This influence contributes to social and economic inequality, conferring an advantage upon certain individuals while imposing a disadvantage upon others. The problem leads to BlackRock's influence being counter-productive for the economy and going against the core values of capitalism. Finally, it's getting worse, we are obliged to find a solution.

What can we do? Are there solutions which would enable us to stay in a capitalist economy and a liberal democracy?

If we consider the capitalist system as the most productive one for an economy, then potential solutions should aim to stay within it. First, let's try to understand why it's the most productive system economically with our current conditions. I'm not saying that capitalism is perfect, it has a lot of defects which we will come back to. However, in our current world and conditions it is the system that works best economically and socially. An example will illustrate this:

Part 4: The future

Let's say you're in charge of the economy, deciding what goods to make and how much they should cost. This task is quite challenging. It involves understanding people's needs, determining production costs, and motivating everyone to contribute. There are three main ways to handle this:

- You can do it poorly, which means setting prices and quantities without accuracy, leading to problems like shortages, long lines for essential items, and corruption.
- You can do it well, but it's tough. Being good at it would likely require using advanced computers to analyse lots of data to help determine the right prices and quantities for everything.
- You can rely on a market. Think of a market as a giant decentralised computer that balances supply and demand. People's preferences act as data, and their transactions determine the prices and quantities of goods. Price is set automatically by supply and demand.

Looking at the different choices. Choice 1 resembles communism as it often exists in practice, while Choice 3 represents capitalism. Choice 2, although appealing, is more like a dream, and the challenge of making it work is known as the "socialist calculation problem", which we won't discuss here. We can imagine that Artificial Intelligence could make it a more viable alternative soon.

Part 4: The future

Capitalism needs a market to work, and that each entity tries to make a profit in that market. So, there is competition between the entities - product competition, service competition or price competition - but what happens if the same person owns these entities? This is a problem that we discussed before: are companies still going to compete against each other if they have the same shareholder whose primary objective is to maximise profits?

If companies engage in fierce competition, potentially causing some to go out of business, the consequence is a reduced income for the common shareholder. When the same shareholder owns multiple entities, it can lead to a situation known as a monopoly or oligopoly, where a single entity or a small number of entities control the market. Would capitalism still work under this framework? If not, what can be done so that it does work?

The first solution, and maybe the easiest one, is to add new laws and regulations.

New antitrust laws, such as the Dodd-Frank Act passed after the financial crisis, could prevent monopolies and promote competition. The Dodd-Frank Act's objective is to protect taxpayers from financial firms, even though it was diluted in 2018. Regulations for index funds could also be enforced more strictly to prevent a single shareholder from owning multiple competing entities. On the other hand, some believe that in a true capitalist system or free market, there should be no antitrust laws.

Changes could also be made to how corporations are run to ensure that they act in the best interests of all stakeholders, not just shareholders. However, similarly to the antitrust law in a "free market", should corporations be told how to operate? It's a difficult question.

Another good option would be to promote competition, providing support for small businesses and startups that are not owned by the same shareholders as their competitors. However, like the two other options, doing that goes against some capitalist ideologies. And in the index funds industries it wouldn't make much sense because there will always be big firms and these big firms will then be included in the ETFs of BlackRock or Vanguard, the same will happen again – concentration of ownership in a few hands, removing competition – which company is in the ETF doesn't really matter.

A problem to consider is that BlackRock, or any other institution that exerts influence through shareholder ownership, will never accept such regulations that could cost them a big share of businesses. As seen before, BlackRock has the power to influence governments and central banks in such a way that new regulations are not set and are avoided. So, regulations are not the solution, governments won't save us, but they may at least help.

Maintaining a balance between allowing businesses to grow and ensuring fair competition is one of the complex challenges of the future. Index funds do benefit average investors and ending them is not the solution, it wouldn't be possible either.

First, what can easily be done is to require greater transparency and disclosure. As John Coates says in his book *The Problem of Twelve*: "One key lament of the regulatory gap is a lack of transparency on how they use their power." He argues that index funds should adapt to the "legal requirements of public consultations that currently apply to government agencies. For index funds, which already are playing a quasi-regulatory role over public companies, these tools should make intuitive sense."

Another of the easier things that can be done is to share the information contained in this book and educate people on such matters. Understanding the problem and being aware of it is already a big step towards a better future where democracy and capitalism would work better. John Adams, the second president of the United States, said in 1765 in a very famous quote: "Liberty cannot be preserved without a general knowledge among the people, who have a right [...] and a desire to know.".

If we all know this problem exists, we will be able to shift to a different economic system where one or a few entities don't control the whole market, or if they do, at least do not exercise their influence and power over us. If everybody is aware of the situation, actions can and will be easily taken to change it. However, if BlackRock stays in the shadows as it is now and people don't speak about the issue, the problem will get worse.

Suppose that investors – the ones investing for retirement – increase their knowledge and understanding of their rights and the impact of their decisions. In that case, they are more likely to exercise their voting rights. This active participation in corporate governance could lead to a more balanced distribution of influence. We could be seeing a democracy inside of index funds. Larry Fink, BlackRock's CEO, is slowly starting to put it into place, but for it to work, people must know that index funds pose a threat to democracy and capitalism, and then they have to take the time to understand the issues that are being voted on, or it will not be a democracy inside index fund but socialism or communism with BlackRock being the managing entity.

In Fink's annual letter to investors, he says: "We continue to innovate in a variety of areas to expand the choices we offer clients. Some of our clients have expressed interest in a more direct role in the stewardship of their capital, and we have sought to deliver solutions that enable them to vote their shares. As I wrote last year to clients and corporate CEOs, I believe that, if widely adopted, voting choice can enhance corporate governance by bringing new voices into shareholder democracy." It is a complicated solution, but if it works, it may reduce the problem that comes with wealth concentration and reduce the influence of these few funds on our lives.

Most importantly to work out the same discussion comes again, people must be aware, if they are aware they will vote their shares. This solution might dilute the influence of the funds in our economic system, but another issue still persists: There is no competition between companies when they are all owned by the same fund.

Part 4: The future

We must lay foundations for the future on which better solutions can be built. Without foundations, our financial system will soon be some sort of unknown communism.

An alternative point of view

What if we changed the perspective on which capitalism is built? Could it work? Capitalism, as traditionally defined, is an economic system where private entities own the means of production. The primary goal of capitalism is profit maximisation, which is achieved through competition and voluntary exchange. However, what if we had a shift towards a more socially conscious form of capitalism? A form in which there is less concentration on profit and more on human needs. Would industries still flourish as in pure capitalism?

This concept is often referred to as "conscious capitalism" or "social capitalism", and it's a model that balances the pursuit of profit with the welfare of all stakeholders, including employees, customers, suppliers, the environment, and the broader community. In this model, businesses still aim to be profitable, but they also take on a broader set of responsibilities towards society.

Some argue that this approach can lead to long-term success by building stronger relationships with customers and employees, improving reputation, and fostering innovation to meet societal needs. However, others argue that it may lead to conflicts of interest and dilute a company's focus on profitability and growth.

Part 4: The future

It is ironic because when you think about it, it looks like the system emerging with index funds today. Of course, index funds want to maximise their profit and the smartest way to achieve that goal is for all the companies in the fund to succeed. Therefore, index funds must look for the common good of each company in the fund, each company must be successful. We previously viewed this as a problem, going against one of the core values of capitalism mentioned by Adam Smith. But what if this problem led us to a better system, where capitalism still focuses on maximising profits, but achieved through the common good of each entity?

Let us imagine that not much change occurs in the next 10-15 years and the Big Three (BlackRock, Vanguard, State Street) become the most influential entities on the planet. Could they shape a better future? What if they became the ones governing the system? Would governments still be useful?

It may well be what will happen, but there are a few problems. First, people must know that the Big Three exert major influence. Therefore, they have to take part and vote their shares, like they were voting for their country's president. In addition, there must be a ruling entity that governs index funds to ensure that social and economic inequality in the speculation of asset prices does not happen. Then, a form of "true democracy" could be established within index funds, where the majority of shareholders have the power to influence company

Part 4: The future

operations and major decisions. It could foster a competitive environment where companies strive to meet the desires of their shareholders. However, this system could also lead to a potential imbalance of influence, with private entities and wealthy individuals wielding more voting power due to their wealth. The objective is not to establish a socialist system where everyone has equal influence. Instead, the aim is to create a system where influence is earned and not concentrated in the hands of a few entities, such as the three major index funds. In this proposed system, those who own more assets will still have a greater influence than those who own less. This is a characteristic of a capitalist system where the wealthy have always had a larger influence on financial markets.

While it may not be possible to completely eliminate this fact, it is feasible to limit it. However, this becomes an ideological issue. Socialists might argue that everyone should have equal voting power, while capitalists might contend that their voting power has been earned through their investments and contributions to the market.

The shared goal is to evolve our current system or create a new one where the influence of index funds in our lives is diminished. Furthermore, this system should continue to work in our favour even in the absence of traditional capitalist competition. This could potentially lead to a more balanced distribution of power and influence in the financial markets, thereby addressing the current issues associated with index funds.

In essence, the challenge is to strike a balance between the capitalist principle of earned influence and the socialist principle of equal influence, while reducing the dominance of index funds and ensuring the system continues to benefit its participants.

This new system could motivate individuals to accumulate wealth in order to gain more influence. In a system where every company is governed by index funds that prioritise the common good, one way to become rich would be to contribute positively to society. We can envision a system where the pursuit of wealth and influence is aligned with the common good creating a form of capitalism that is more responsive to the needs and wants of the majority. However, this new system would need to carefully manage the potential for wealth concentration and ensure a fair balance of influence, or the same will happen again.

Larry Fink confirms in his 2023 Annual Chairman's Letter to Investors, the importance of optimism and trust in the financial system: "Long-term investing requires trust in the financial system and a fundamental belief that tomorrow will be better than today. We need leaders today who will give people reasons to be hopeful, who can articulate a vision for a brighter future. And, we need institutions that inspire trust. So much of what we have lost over the past few years – through Covid, war in Europe, political polarization, geopolitical fragmentation, and macro-economic shifts – has eroded optimism, trust, and a belief in a better future."

Part 4: The future

If we want a sound financial system, we need institutions that inspire trust and leaders that can guarantee that trust. Could the index fund firms fulfil those requirements in the future? Would Larry Fink become the next president of the World? Would you trust him?

If not, are we even capable of putting an end to the immense power of index funds?

To conclude

To conclude

A few things to remember

BlackRock has many investments that hedge others in the event of a crisis. We have seen the example of COVID-19, but there are many others, such as the war in the Ukraine which has had a big impact on BlackRock's investments in the energy sector. However, because BlackRock's energy investments are so diversified, it has not lost money. If its Russian energy investments perform poorly, its other investments perform better than usual because the demand is still the same. BlackRock has investments in almost all industries and owns shares of all the most important players in each sector. BlackRock is too big to fail because of that, and it would be challenging for BlackRock to actually fail. The Big Three have become like a colossal iceberg, unseen beneath the surface, yet so massive that their movements steer the currents of the global economy.

We have also seen that BlackRock possesses the capacity to influence a company's decisions in a manner that may ultimately serve the interests of other entities within its ownership portfolio and has already done so in the past. Furthermore, the sheer size of BlackRock's holdings gives it the ability to impact market prices and liquidity. BlackRock's success is closely tracked by other market participants, meaning that its actions and decisions can have broader implications for the financial system's stability.

To conclude

Ultimately, BlackRock poses a significant challenge to both free markets and democratic principles. While opinions on this matter vary, some argue that competition between companies can persist even with a common shareholder advocating for the collective good. However, this perspective overlooks a crucial concern: as the influence of common shareholders like BlackRock grows, it becomes increasingly difficult for companies to ignore their interests. Inevitably, this trend could reach a point where the sheer size of these shareholders' stakes renders competition among companies useless. The dominance of major shareholders such as the Big Three not only diminishes the ability of companies to compete effectively but also consolidates significant voting power, further solidifying their control over corporate decision-making.

Capitalism relies on healthy competition, but with major players like BlackRock having significant influence, true competition diminishes. Additionally, free markets require minimal intervention between buyers and sellers. While past concerns focused on government intervention, the real threat now comes from index fund managers like BlackRock. This undermines democracy as a few individuals wield immense power over the economic system, potentially distorting markets and eroding democratic principles.

BlackRock influences economic and social inequality, but not because it prioritises profits over social and environmental responsibility. BlackRock does care about ESG. It influences inequality because some people have

To conclude

access to its service or software, Aladdin, and others do not. Thus, BlackRock creates inequality by having created a monopoly around itself. The worst BlackRock services are primarily accessible to individuals who are already affluent and have significant economic influence. This exclusivity amplifies their financial capabilities and resources, exacerbating the existing wealth disparity in our society. In essence, BlackRock inadvertently acts as a catalyst that further empowers the wealthy, leaving the less privileged at a disadvantage, widening the wealth gap.

Indeed, there is a silver lining as individuals from the lower economic strata are gradually beginning to invest their money. This trend is a positive step towards financial literacy and independence. However, this also implies that the value and influence of index funds will continue to grow. While this growth can lead to increased returns for investors, it also means that these financial instruments will wield even more power in the economy, putting an end to the capitalism system.

Our system has become governed by a small number of entities with considerable influence. We must look for solutions. We must share the problem for people to understand it. We must acknowledge that the index funds' influence won't be easy to undermine. A new system, with democracy inside index funds and index funds governing for the common good, is much more probable. Therefore, we must first work towards a common understanding of the problem that index funds have created.

Acknowledgement

The hardest part is that I still have the impression that I haven't said everything important there is to say and that something is missing. This work is not a finished product. There is still much to discover and many topics that need to be addressed to understand our economic system and how it works.

I would like to thank all the people that take the time to spread this knowledge and information, without the articles, the research paper, and the few books this book wouldn't have been possible.

I would like to thank the people that read and reviewed this book and helped me write it.

My aim with this book was to spread knowledge and learn something in the process. We should all aim to understand more of what is happening around us.

I hope that you have learned something from reading this. That is, for me, the most important objective.

Special thanks to my mother, I would have never accomplished such a project without her support.

References

Beginning to part 1 (alphabetic order):

About BlackRock in Switzerland. (2022, June). BlackRock. https://www.blackrock.com/ch/individual/en/about-us/about-blackrock

Baldwin, W. (n.d.). John Bogle and the Cost of Mutual Funds. Forbes. Retrieved December 2, 2023, from https://www.forbes.com/forbes/2010/0913/opinions-william-baldwin-sidelines-mostly-right-jack-bogle.html

Beagley, A. (2021, February 19). Why was the Bank of England founded? Www.bankofengland.co.uk. https://www.bankofengland.co.uk/museum/online-collections/blog/why-was-the-bank-of-england-founded

Beattie, A. (2020, April 5). The Birth of Stock Exchanges. Investopedia. https://www.investopedia.com/articles/07/stock-exchange-history.asp

Beattie, A. (2023, December 18). The Evolution of Stock Exchanges. Investopedia. https://www.investopedia.com/articles/07/stock-exchange-history.asp#citation-10

BlackRock Shareholders | Who Owns The Most Shares of BlackRock? (n.d.). Capital.com. Retrieved August 2023, from https://capital.com/blackrock-shareholder-who-owns-most-blk-stock

Bordo, M. D. (2007). A Brief History of Central Banks. Economic Commentary, 12/1/2007. https://www.clevelandfed.org/en/publications/economic-commentary/2007/ec-20071201-a-brief-history-of-central-banks

Coates, J. (2023). The Problem of Twelve (pp. 39–42). Columbia.

Colagrossi, M. (2018, July 8). How the Medici family created and lost their banking empire. Big Think. https://bigthink.com/culture-religion/how-the-medici-family-created-and-lost-their-banking-empire/

Culloton, D. (2011, August 9). A Brief History of Indexing. Morningstar, Inc. https://www.morningstar.com/articles/390749/a-brief-history-of-indexing

Famous Quotations on Banking. (n.d.). The Money Masters. Retrieved February 1, 2024, from http://www.themoneymasters.com/the-money-masters/famous-quotations-on-banking/

Georgieva, K. (2022, February 9). The Future of Money: Gearing up for Central Bank Digital Currency.

International Monetary Fund. https://www.imf.org/en/News/Articles/2022/02/09/sp020922-the-future-of-money-gearing-up-for-central-bank-digital-currency

HILDRETH, R. (2001). The History of Banks. Social History of Medicine, 14(2). https://doi.org/10.1093/shm/14.2.363

History Sveriges Riksbank. (2015). Riksbank.se. https://www.riksbank.se/en-gb/about-the-riksbank/history/

History.com Editors. (2009, November 9). John Locke. HISTORY. https://www.history.com/topics/european-history/john-locke

History.com Editors. (2018, August 21). The Medici Family. HISTORY; A&E Television Networks. https://www.history.com/topics/renaissance/medici-family

How Banks Create Money - Positive Money. (2013). Positive Money. https://positivemoney.org/how-money-%20works/how-banks-%20create-money/#:~:text=Most%20of%20the%20money%20in

International Monetary Fund. (2023, April). Report for Selected Countries and Subjects. IMF. https://www.imf.org/en/Publications/WEO/weo-database/2023/April/weo-report?c=111

INTERNATIONAL MONETARY FUND Understanding Financial Interconnectedness Prepared by the Strategy, Policy, and Review Department and the Monetary and Capital Markets Department, in collaboration with the Statistics Department and in consultation with other Departments. (2010). https://www.imf.org/external/np/pp/eng/2010/100410.pdf

J.Colley, L. (n.d.). United Kingdom - The Napoleonic Wars. Encyclopedia Britannica. Retrieved January 2024, from https://www.britannica.com/place/United-Kingdom/The-Napoleonic-Wars

Koller, C. (2022, November 18). Fiat Money simply explained. Pocket Ethereum. https://pocketethereum.com/learn/economy/fiatmoney-explained

Lauria, P. (2022, July 31). Who Was John Locke? Investopedia. https://www.investopedia.com/john-locke-5271458

Leonard, C. (2022). The lords of easy money : how the Federal Reserve broke the American economy (pp.115, 116). Simon & Schuster.

Leonard, C. (2022). The lords of easy money : how the Federal Reserve broke the American economy (p.119). Simon & Schuster.

Lexical Investigations: Fiat. (2013, August 13). Dictionary.com. https://www.dictionary.com/e/fiat/

List of regions by past GDP (PPP). (2024, March 29). Wikipedia. https://en.wikipedia.org/wiki/List_of_regions_by_past_GDP_(PPP)#cite_ref-maddison_4-2

Liu, Z., Quiet, S., & Roth, B. (2015). Banking sector interconnectedness: what is it, how can we measure it and why does it matter? Bank of England Quarterly Bulletin, 55(2), 130–138.

Moore, A. (2015, March 25). Bank of England History. Intriguing History. https://intriguing-history.com/bank-of-england-history/

Nevil, S. (2023, March 28). Fractional Reserve Banking. Investopedia. https://www.investopedia.com/terms/f/fractionalreservebanking.asp

Nicki Lisa Cole . (2019, July 3). The Globalization of Capitalism. ThoughtCo. https://www.thoughtco.com/globalization-of-capitalism-3026076

Paterson, W., & Godfrey, M. (1694). A brief account of the intended Bank of England.

https://quod.lib.umich.edu/e/eebo/A56581.0001.001/1:2?rgn=div1

Petty impressive. (2013, December 21). The Economist. https://www.economist.com/finance-and-economics/2013/12/21/petty-impressive

Photographer: Joel Saget. (2023, October 19). Larry Fink Leads CEOs Back to COP Talks They Snubbed Last Year. Bloomberg.com. https://www.bloomberg.com/news/articles/2023-10-19/larry-fink-leads-ceos-back-to-cop-talks-they-snubbed-last-year

Preqin. (n.d.). History of the Hedge Fund Industry | Preqin. Www.preqin.com. Retrieved August 6, 2023, from https://www.preqin.com/academy/lesson-3-hedge-funds/history-of-the-hedge-fund-industry#:~:text=1960s%3A%20Rise%20of%20the%20Hedge%20Fund&text=In%201969%2C%20the%20first%20fund

Process of Credit Creation by Commercial Banks - Law Corner. (2021, February 6). https://lawcorner.in/process-of-credit-creation-by-commercial-banks/

Rain, T. B. (2019, March 12). Alfred Winslow Jones: The Father of the Hedge Fund Industry. Medium. https://tradingroomshq.medium.com/alfred-winslow-jones-the-father-of-the-hedge-fund-industry-698d069c0d53

Sharma, R. (2022, April 11). Adam Smith: The Father of Economics. Investopedia. https://www.investopedia.com/updates/adam-smith-economics/

The Editors of Encyclopaedia Britannica. (2023, June 16). Mercantilism | Definition & Examples | Britannica Money. Www.britannica.com. https://www.britannica.com/money/topic/mercantilism

The Fed - What is the purpose of the Federal Reserve System? (2016, November 3). Board of Governors of the Federal Reserve System. https://www.federalreserve.gov/faqs/about_12594.htm#:~:text=It%20was%20created%20by%20the

Tomes, L. (2021, January 15). The History of Income Tax in the UK. History Hit. https://www.historyhit.com/income-tax-history-uk/

Understanding Fiat Money: What It Is, How It Works? (2023, January 24). FinFormed. https://www.finformed.org/understanding-fiat-money-what-it-is-how-it-works-examples-advantages-and-disadvantages/

Ungarino, R. (2020, December 2). Here are 9 fascinating facts to know about BlackRock, the world's largest asset manager. Business Insider. https://www.businessinsider.com/what-to-know-about-blackrock-larry-fink-biden-cabinet-facts-2020-12?r=US&IR=T

Value of 1815 British pounds today | UK Inflation Calculator. (n.d.). Www.in2013dollars.com. Retrieved January 11, 2024, from https://www.in2013dollars.com/uk/inflation/1815

Wigglesworth, R. (2021, July 19). Massive passive: 50 years of the index fund. Www.ft.com. https://www.ft.com/content/a2e11698-88de-4fe9-a05f-dc618fed0f23

Wikipedia, 1787 portrait. (2019, March 9). Adam Smith. Wikipedia; Wikimedia Foundation. https://en.wikipedia.org/wiki/Adam_Smith

Wikipedia Contributors. (2019, March 18). Central bank. Wikipedia; Wikimedia Foundation. https://en.wikipedia.org/wiki/Central_bank

Wikipedia Contributors. (2024, January 15). William Paterson (banker). Wikipedia; Wikimedia Foundation. https://en.wikipedia.org/wiki/William_Paterson_%28banker%29

Wikipedia, Marx in 1875. (2019, January 10). Karl Marx. Wikipedia; Wikimedia Foundation. https://en.wikipedia.org/wiki/Karl_Marx

Wikipedia, T. original uploader was T. at E. (2005, June 16). English: Enlargement of the 20-dollar bill. Enlargements conform with American copyright law if they show only small parts of the bill. Wikimedia Commons. https://commons.wikimedia.org/wiki/File:1in_god_we_trust.jpg

Wisdom, Q. (2023, July 17). Adam Smith: 10 Insights from the Father of Economics. Medium; Medium. https://medium.com/@quoteswisdom/adam-smith-10-insights-from-the-father-of-economics-59c1fa1c6f8c

Worldometer. (2023). World Population by Year - Worldometers. Worldometers.info. https://www.worldometers.info/world-population/world-population-by-year/

Part 2 (alphabetic order):

Email conversation between Blackrock and the Treasury department, The New York Times. (2020, March). https://int.nyt.com/data/documenttools/black-rock-emails-march-april-2020/dde950256eaa64f7/full.pdf

Bastardo, J. (2023, July 23). BlackRock's ETF Can Change The Bitcoin Game After Years Of SEC Rejections. Forbes. https://www.forbes.com/sites/digital-assets/2023/07/23/blackrocks-etf-can-change-the-bitcoin-game-after-years-of-sec-rejections/?sh=756e5b241b8b

BBC NEWS. (2018, October 15). Saudi Arabia: Five reasons why Gulf kingdom matters to the West. BBC News. https://www.bbc.com/news/world-middle-east-45861708

BlackRock. (2020, March 31). History. BlackRock. https://www.blackrock.com/corporate/about-us/blackrock-history

BlackRock. (2023). BLK-4Q23-Earnings-Release.pdf. https://s24.q4cdn.com/856567660/files/doc_financials/2023/Q4/BLK-4Q23-Earnings-Release.pdf

BlackRock, Inc. - Stock Information - Stock Quote & Chart. (n.d.). Ir.blackrock.com. Retrieved September 21, 2023, from https://ir.blackrock.com/stock-information/stock-quote-and-chart/default.aspx

Blakeley, G. (2021, June 11). How Capitalism Concentrates Power. Tribunemag.co.uk. https://tribunemag.co.uk/2021/06/how-capitalism-concentrates-power/

Brush, S. (2023, August 15). BlackRock, Fund Managers Brace for Even More Scrutiny Over China. Bloomberg.com. https://www.bloomberg.com/news/articles/2023-08-15/blackrock-fund-managers-brace-for-even-more-scrutiny-over-china

Dividends, M. (2023, September 13). BlackRock: A Dividend Growth Compounder You Do Not Want To Miss. Seeking Alpha. https://seekingalpha.com/article/4634817-blackrock-a-dividend-growth-compounder-you-do-not-want-to-miss

Federal Deposit Insurance Corporation, List of Awards and Contractor Contact Information. (2022, May). https://www.fdic.gov/about/doing-business/awards-contractor-contact-info-financial-services.pdf

Fidelity International. (2023, November 21). Www.fidelity.lu. https://www.fidelity.lu/articles/analysis-and-research/2023-11-21-2024-etf-market-outlook-outlook-2024-1700552749551

Financial Markets Advisory (FMA). (n.d.). BlackRock. Retrieved February 2, 2024, from https://www.blackrock.com/financial-markets-advisory

Fintel Staff. (2023, February 7). BlackRock Increases Position in Lockheed Martin (LMT). Nasdaq.com. https://www.nasdaq.com/articles/blackrock-increases-position-in-lockheed-martin-lmt

Foroohar, K., & Vidya, S. (2009, May 8). BlackRock Is Go-To Firm to Divine Wall Street Assets. Bloomberg.com. https://www.bloomberg.com/news/articles/2009-05-08/blackrock-is-go-to-firm-to-divine-wall-street-assets

Gittelsohn, J. (2019, September 11). End of Era: Passive Equity Funds Surpass Active in Epic Shift. Bloomberg.com. https://www.bloomberg.com/news/articles/2019-09-11/passive-u-s-equity-funds-eclipse-active-in-epic-industry-shift

Goldstein, M. (2020, March 25). The Fed Asks for BlackRock's Help in an Echo of 2008. The New York Times. https://www.nytimes.com/2020/03/25/business/blackrock-federal-reserve.html

Henderson, R., & Walker, O. (2020, February 24). Subscribe to read | Financial Times. Www.ft.com. https://www.ft.com/content/5ba6f40e-4e4d-11ea-95a0-43d18ec715f5

Hunnicutt, T. (2017, October 10). BlackRock hires former Obama climate adviser: memo. Reuters. https://www.reuters.com/article/us-blackrock-moves-brian-deese-idUSKBN1CF2GS/

Hunnicutt, T. (2019, February 13). BlackRock hires former Fed official Fischer as an adviser: memo. Reuters. https://finance.yahoo.com/news/blackrock-hires-former-fed-official-160239116.html?guccounter=1&guce_referrer=aHR0cHM6Ly93d3cuYmluZy5jb20v&guce_referrer_sig=AQAAANDIJKKEKLyHvnieNpHCe1bJeI8CYUvIlFzap0pFw

UVppwK59Kx75HgahYVVe8akobbab-o2r9Cn-AevwQcUJqGqw0X6YsAEZXDFsE0dUt_1OPiqEVaRwaOwiPmoZNzBfL1OaPLM_oWdpwF8MoHuDp9-KBtWZ95Iw1O_KRJe5Frl

Investing in Israel | Asset management. (2015, February). BlackRock. https://www.blackrock.com/il/intermediaries/en/themes/ishares-etf

Investing in Israel | Asset management. (2019, September 30). BlackRock. https://www.blackrock.com/il/intermediaries/en/etfs-and-indexing/visualizing-the-expanse-etf-universe

Johnson, L. (2024, January 16). BlackRock buys Global Infrastructure Partners, makes $12.5B bet on infrastructure market. ESG Dive. https://www.esgdive.com/news/blackrock-buys-global-infrastructure-partners-125b-decarbonization-transition/704616/#:~:text=BlackRock%2C%20the%20nation

Justice, D. (2022, April 12). BlackRock could make 110% profit out of Zambia's debt crisis. International Debt Charity | Debt Justice (Formerly Jubilee Debt Campaign). https://debtjustice.org.uk/press-release/blackrock-could-make-110-profit-out-of-zambias-debt-crisis

Largest ETF Providers by Assets Under Management. (n.d.). Stock Analysis. Retrieved June 2, 2023, from https://stockanalysis.com/etf/provider/

Larry Fink's Annual 2022 Letter to CEOs. (2022). BlackRock. https://www.blackrock.com/corporate/investor-relations/larry-fink-ceo-letter#:~:text=Capitalism%20has%20the%20power%20to

Leung, C. (2023, September 15). BlackRock China funds named in US lawmaker probe suffer outflows. Financial Times. https://www.ft.com/content/6fa5293e-2df9-42ca-9f2a-7f6e857d9992

Masters, B. (2023, June 19). BlackRock and JPMorgan help set up Ukraine reconstruction bank. Financial Times. https://www.ft.com/content/3d6041fb-5747-4564-9874-691742aa52a2

Michelle Price. (2023, September 6). Grayscale urges U.S. SEC to approve spot bitcoin ETF following court victory. Reuters. https://www.reuters.com/business/finance/grayscale-urges-us-sec-approve-spot-bitcoin-etf-following-court-victory-2023-09-05/#:~:text=The%20SEC%20has%20denied%20all,protect%20investors%20from%20market%20manipulation

Ministry of Defense @Israel_MOD. (2021, December 31). Twitter.com. https://x.com/Israel_MOD/status/1476820276239388678?s=20

Ministry of Economy of Ukraine. (2022, December 3). ShieldSquare Captcha. Www.kmu.gov.ua. https://www.kmu.gov.ua/en/news/masovyi-prytik-priamykh-inozemnykh-investytsii-v-ukrainu-ie-nemynuchym-oleksandr-hryban-na-ukrainian-infrastructure-forum-u-londoni

Pouille , J. (2019, April 17). Blackrock: The financial leviathan that bears down on Europe's decisions. Investigate Europe. https://www.investigate-europe.eu/en/posts/blackrock-the-financial-leviathan-that-bears-down-on-europes-decisions

Reichl, D., & Brush , S. (2023, April 5). BlackRock Hired to Sell $114 Billion in Failed Banks' Securities. Bloomberg.com. https://www.bloomberg.com/news/articles/2023-04-05/blackrock-hired-to-sell-114-billion-in-failed-banks-securities

Reichl, D., & Brush, S. (2023, April 5). BlackRock Hired to Sell $114 Billion in Failed Banks' Securities. Bloomberg.com. https://www.bloomberg.com/news/articles/2023-04-05/blackrock-hired-to-sell-114-billion-in-failed-banks-securities

Reuters. (2022, November 14). Saudi wealth fund, BlackRock to jointly explore Mideast infrastructure projects. Yahoo Finance. https://finance.yahoo.com/news/saudi-wealth-fund-blackrock-jointly-090119785.html

Smialek, J. (2021, June 24). Top U.S. Officials Consulted With BlackRock as Markets Melted Down. The New York Times. https://www.nytimes.com/2021/06/24/business/economy/fed-blackrock-pandemic-crisis.html

Staff Writer and Reuters. (2022, November 14). PIF and BlackRock to explore Gulf infrastructure projects. AGBI. https://www.agbi.com/article/pif-and-blackrock-to-explore-middle-east-infrastructure-projects/

Statista Research Department. (2023, September 14). BlackRock: assets under management 2021. Statista. https://www.statista.com/statistics/891292/assets-under-management-blackrock/

TGH Editorial Team. (2023, January 7). BlackRock: A Journey From Startup To Global Conglomerate | The Global Hues. BlackRock: A Journey from Startup to Global Conglomerate. https://theglobalhues.com/blackrock-a-journey-from-startup-to-global-conglomerate/#:~:text=In%202009%2C%20BlackRock%20has%20made

The UN. (2023, April). A world of debt: Regional stories | UNCTAD. Unctad.org. https://unctad.org/publication/world-of-debt/regional-stories

TheBitTimes. (2024, January 17). Guest Post by TheBitTimes: Bitcoin ETFs Erupt With "Insane" Volumes 3X Greater Than All 500 ETFs Launched In 2023 Combined | CoinMarketCap. Coinmarketcap.com. https://coinmarketcap.com/community/articles/65a7c970b80a051ab94cb517/

Ungarino, R. (2020, December 2). Here are 9 fascinating facts to know about BlackRock, the world's largest asset manager. Business Insider. https://www.businessinsider.com/what-to-know-about-blackrock-larry-fink-biden-cabinet-facts-2020-12?r=US&IR=T

Vaughan, A. (2023, January 7). BlackRock: A Journey From Startup To Global Conglomerate | The Global Hues. BlackRock Is the Biggest Company You've Never Heard Of. https://theglobalhues.com/blackrock-a-journey-from-startup-to-global-conglomerate/#:~:text=In%202009%2C%20BlackRock%20has%20made

Walsh, S. (2022, December 28). Zelensky, BlackRock CEO agree to coordinate Ukraine rebuilding investment - UPI.com. UPI. https://www.upi.com/Top_News/World-

News/2022/12/28/ukraine-Zelensky-BlackRock-CEO-agree-rebuild-investment/3961672265216/

Watson, R. (2024, January 11). BlackRock's new spot bitcoin ETF tops $1 billion in big first day of trading. The Block. https://www.theblock.co/post/272123/blackrocks-new-spot-bitcoin-etf-tops-1-billion-in-big-first-day-of-trading

Part 3 (alphabetic order):

Image courtesy of Roles and Responsibilities of Federal Reserve Directors, a Federal Reserve System publication. (n.d.). https://www.federalreserve.gov/aboutthefed/directors/pdf/roles_responsibilities_FINALweb013013.pdf

adam. (2022, June 30). ESG and the Investment World's 12 Emperors – Corporate Citizenship Project. Corporate Citizenship Project. https://corporatecitizenshipproject.com/esg-and-the-investment-worlds-12-emperors/

BankUnderground. (2019, October 18). The ownership of central banks. Bank Underground. https://bankunderground.co.uk/2019/10/18/the-ownership-of-central-banks/

Birchall, S. (2022, October 4). BlackRock's Impact Opportunities Fund dives into the education sector. New Private Markets.

https://www.newprivatemarkets.com/blackrocks-impact-opportunities-fund-dives-into-the-education-sector/

BlackRock. (2022, November). Empowering investors through Voting Choice. BlackRock (Pdf). https://www.blackrock.com/corporate/literature/publication/voting-choice-factsheet.pdf

BlackRock. (2023). 2023 Investment Stewardship Voting Spotlight. https://www.blackrock.com/corporate/literature/publication/2023-investment-stewardship-voting-spotlight.pdf

BlackRock. (2024). BlackRock Investment Stewardship Engagement Priorities Summary. https://www.blackrock.com/corporate/literature/publication/blk-stewardship-priorities-final.pdf

BlackRock Equity Dividend Fund | Weapon investments | Weapon Free Funds. (2023, June 30). BlackRock Equity Dividend Fund | Weapon Investments | Weapon Free Funds. https://weaponfreefunds.org/fund/blackrock-equity-dividend-fund/MADVX/weapon-investments/FSUSA001M1/FOUSA00DTN

BlackRock Investments in Switzerland. (2022). Spotlight on BlackRock. https://spotlightonblackrock.ch/en/data/updated-investments

Bogle, J. C. (2018, November 29). Bogle Sounds a Warning on Index Funds. Wall Street Journal. https://www.wsj.com/articles/bogle-sounds-a-warning-on-index-funds-1543504551

Brush, S., & Allison, B. (2022, November 4). BlackRock Spends Record on US Political Campaigns as ESG Fight Intensifies. Bloomberg.com. https://www.bloomberg.com/news/articles/2022-11-04/blackrock-spends-record-amount-on-us-political-campaigns-amid-esg-fallout

Bubb, R., & Catan, E. (2020). The Party Structure of Mutual Funds. ECGI Working Paper Series in Law. https://deliverypdf.ssrn.com/delivery.php?ID=365086110124001111024087004066118029031084070081044092070071068070127099105091071113057037031013031061114092093020083108074074015055013006080118014011081108123097095024042036093119120119001071084097070009005015067005071125097077009090029000120125026001&EXT=pdf&INDEX=TRUE

Carter, R. (2023, February 16). How Much Money Is in Circulation in 2023. Moneytransfers.com. https://moneytransfers.com/news/2022/06/12/how-much-money-is-in-circulation

Chakraborty, V., & Gull, Z. (2023, April 4). Vanguard, BlackRock are the top investors in US banks. Www.spglobal.com. https://www.spglobal.com/marketintelligence/en/news-insights/latest-news-headlines/vanguard-blackrock-are-the-top-investors-in-us-banks-74959785

Chitinis, O. (2023, March 27). Giant conglomerate's that control the world!!... Www.linkedin.com. https://www.linkedin.com/pulse/giant-conglomerates-control-world-omkar-chitnis

Donnelly, C., & Chakrabarti, M. (2023, August 7). Are index funds getting too powerful? Www.wbur.org. https://www.wbur.org/onpoint/2023/08/07/how-index-funds-are-shaping-corporations-and-the-american-economy

Fink, L. (2023). Larry Fink's Annual Chairman's Letter to Investors. BlackRock. https://www.blackrock.com/corporate/investor-relations/larry-fink-annual-chairmans-letter

Griffin, C. (2020, July 20). Margins: Estimating the Influence of the Big Three on Shareholder Proposals. Blogs.law.ox.ac.uk. https://blogs.law.ox.ac.uk/business-law-blog/blog/2020/07/margins-estimating-influence-big-three-shareholder-proposals

Griffith, S., & Lund, D. (2019). CONFLICTED MUTUAL FUND VOTING IN CORPORATE LAW. https://www.bu.edu/bulawreview/files/2019/06/GRIFFITH-LUND.pdf

Heemskerk, E., Fichtner, J., & Garcia-Bernardo, J. (2017, May 10). These three firms own corporate America. The Conversation. https://theconversation.com/these-three-firms-own-corporate-america-77072

Henderson, R., & Walker, O. (2020, February 24). Subscribe to read | Financial Times. Www.ft.com. https://www.ft.com/content/5ba6f40e-4e4d-11ea-95a0-43d18ec715f5

Levine, M. (2020, July 23). Money Stuff: You Don't Need Profits Anymore. Bloomberg.com. https://www.bloomberg.com/news/newsletters/2020-07-23/money-stuff-you-don-t-need-profits-anymore

Lu, M. (2023, June 20). Visualizing BlackRock's Top Equity Holdings. Visualcapitalist.com. https://www.visualcapitalist.com/blackrocks-top-equity-holdings-2023/#:~:text=As%20expected%2C%20BlackRock%27s%20top%20equity,America%27s%20two%20largest%20semiconductor%20companies

Market Share: Country Comparison. (2022). Spotlight on BlackRock. https://spotlightonblackrock.ch/en/data/country-comparison

McLaughlin, D., & Massa, A. (2020, January 9). The Hidden Dangers of the Great Index Fund Takeover.

Bloomberg.com. https://www.bloomberg.com/news/features/2020-01-09/the-hidden-dangers-of-the-great-index-fund-takeover

Neal, J. (2023, August 24). Harvard Law professor explains why private equity and index funds need reform. Harvard Law School. https://hls.harvard.edu/today/harvard-law-professor-explains-why-private-equity-and-index-funds-need-reform/

Nguyen, L., & Jessop, S. (2023, January 17). Davos 2023: BlackRock U.S. inflows dwarf $4 bln lost in ESG backlash -CEO. Reuters. https://www.reuters.com/business/finance/davos-2023-blackrock-us-inflows-dwarf-4-bln-lost-esg-backlash-ceo-2023-01-17/

Norton, L. P. (2020, June 1). BlackRock Is Biggest Beneficiary of Fed Purchases of Corporate Bond ETFs. Www.barrons.com. https://www.barrons.com/amp/articles/blackrock-is-biggest-beneficiary-of-fed-purchases-of-corporate-bond-etfs-51591034726

Phillips, M. (2021, June 9). Exxon's Board Defeat Signals the Rise of Social-Good Activists. The New York Times. https://www.nytimes.com/2021/06/09/business/exxon-mobil-engine-no1-activist.html

Potter, S. (2021, July 20). BlackRock-Led "Big Three" May Forestall Chaos in Stock Markets. Bloomberg.com. https://www.bloomberg.com/news/articles/2021-07-20/blackrock-led-big-three-may-forestall-chaos-in-stock-markets#xj4y7vzkg

Schmitt, W. (2024, March 24). US investment funds pull $13.3bn from BlackRock in anti-ESG campaign. Www.ft.com. https://www.ft.com/content/9306c8f2-530d-45ca-a830-4d26e5a90509

Simpson, C., & Kishan, S. (2021, December 31). Bloomberg - Are you a robot? Www.bloomberg.com. https://www.bloomberg.com/news/articles/2021-12-31/how-blackrock-s-invisible-hand-helped-make-esg-a-hot-ticket

Strine, L. E. (2019). Fiduciary Blind Spot: The Failure of Institutional Investors to Prevent the Illegitimate Use of Working Americans' Savings for Corporate Political Spending. SSRN Electronic Journal. https://doi.org/10.2139/ssrn.3304611

Swiss National Bank. (2022, July 4). Breakdown of share ownership . Www.snb.ch. https://www.snb.ch/en/mmr/reference/shares_structure/source/shares_structure.en.pdf. (PDF).

TGH Editorial Team. (2023, January 7). BlackRock: A Journey From Startup To Global Conglomerate | The Global Hues. https://theglobalhues.com/blackrock-a-journey-from-startup-to-global-conglomerate/#:~:text=In%202009%2C%20BlackRock%20has%20made

Total net assets of U.S. ETFs 2002-2020. (2023, July 12). Statista. https://www.statista.com/statistics/295632/etf-us-net-assets/

Vanguard. (2023). Vanguard in a nutshell. https://www.ch.vanguard/content/dam/intl/europe/documents/en/vanguard-in-a-nutshell-eu-en.pdf

Vaughan, A. (2022, July 8). BlackRock is the Biggest Company You've Never Heard of. Innovation & Tech Today. https://innotechtoday.com/blackrock-is-the-biggest-company-youve-never-heard-of/

Part 4 (alphabetic order):

2022 Larry fink CEO letter - Letters. (2022). BlackRock. https://www.blackrock.com/dk/intermediaries/2022-larry-fink-ceo-letter#:~:text=This%20is%20the%20power%20of

Ackerman, S. (2017, October 24). Finance isn't just an industry. It's a system of social control. Jacobin.com. https://jacobin.com/2017/10/finance-capital-shareholders-profit-market

Adamczyk, A. (2019, September 19). Index funds are more popular than ever—here's why they're a smart investment. CNBC; CNBC. https://www.cnbc.com/2019/09/19/why-index-funds-are-a-smart-investment.html

Adams, J. (1765). A Dissertation on the Canon and Feudal Law . https://www.oxfordreference.com/display/10.1093/acref/9780191826719.001.0001/q-oro-ed4-00000046#:~:text=Liberty%20cannot%20be%20preserved%20without,and%20conduct%20of%20their%20rulers.

Bailey, R. E., Davies, G., & Chown, J. (1995). A History of Money: From Ancient Times to the Present Day. The Economic Journal, 105(430), 9–11. https://doi.org/10.2307/2235045

Bebchuk Lucian A, & Hirst, S. (2022, December 12). Big Three Power, and Why it Matters. Ssrn.com. https://papers.ssrn.com/sol3/papers.cfm?abstract_id=4300447

Bebchuk, L. A., & Hirst, S. (2019). The Specter of the Giant Three. SSRN Electronic Journal, 99:721. https://doi.org/10.2139/ssrn.3385501

Capital Magazine. (n.d.). Antitrust & Monopolies. Capitalism Magazine. https://www.capitalismmagazine.com/markets/antitrust/

Coates, J. (2023). The Problem of Twelve (p. 132). Columbia.

Coates, J. (2023). The Problem of Twelve (p. 130). Columbia.

Fink, L. (2023). Larry Fink's Annual Chairman's Letter to Investors. BlackRock. https://www.blackrock.com/corporate/investor-relations/larry-fink-annual-chairmans-letter

Hayes, A. (2023, April 26). Dodd-Frank Wall Street Reform and Consumer Protection Act . Investopedia. https://www.investopedia.com/terms/d/dodd-frank-financial-regulatory-reform-bill.asp

Levine, M. (2016, August 24). Are Index Funds Communist? Bloomberg.com. https://www.bloomberg.com/opinion/articles/2016-08-24/are-index-funds-communist?sref=1kJVNqnU

Levine, M. (2020, July 23). Money Stuff: You Don't Need Profits Anymore. Bloomberg.com. https://www.bloomberg.com/news/newsletters/2020-07-23/money-stuff-you-don-t-need-profits-anymore

Smith, A. (1776). The Wealth of Nations. W. Strahan and T. Cadell. book 4, chapter 3.

Wikipedia Contributors. (2019, January 10). Karl Marx. Wikipedia; Wikimedia Foundation. https://en.wikipedia.org/wiki/Karl_Marx. Photo: Photograph by John Mayall, 1875.

Thank you

Contact Alessandro Moneta: aleemoneta@gmail.com

www.ingramcontent.com/pod-product-compliance
Lightning Source LLC
Chambersburg PA
CBHW071207240526
45470CB00018B/1535